CRITERES

SOLACE

SOLACE
The Missing Dimension in Psychiatry

Paul C. Horton, M.D.

The University of Chicago Press
Chicago and London

To Kathy, Paul, and Alex

PAUL C. HORTON, M.D., a psychiatrist in
private practice in Connecticut, has held teach-
ing appointments in the School of Medicine of
both Yale University and the University of
Connecticut. He has published numerous
articles in professional journals.

The University of Chicago Press, Chicago 60637
The University of Chicago Press, Ltd., London

Library of Congress Cataloging in Publication Data

Horton, Paul C.
  Solace: The missing dimension in psychiatry.

  Bibliography: p.
  Includes index.
  1. Psychiatry—Philosophy. 2. Psychotherapy—
Philosophy. 3. Consolation. 4. Object (Philosophy)
—Psychological aspects. 5. Developmental
psychology. 6. Maturation (Psychology) I. Title.
[DNLM: 1. Defense mechanisms. 2. Human development.
WM 193 H823v]
RC437.5.H67   616.89'001   81-2794
ISBN 0-226-35386-9   AACR2

Contents

Acknowledgments

Henry Coppolillo, M.D., introduced me to the transitional object concept. His article, "maturational aspects of the transitional phenomenon" was at least a decade ahead of its time. The many discussions that he and I had regarding the nature of transitional relatedness contributed greatly to my understanding. Paul Arkema, M.D., was of special assistance with the manuscript. His comments on rough drafts several times had virtual interpretive value. In addition to suggesting changes that led to greater clarity, he wrote four case reports and permitted me to use an illustrative case from his article (1981) on the borderline syndrome and transitional relatedness. Professor Jerome Ellison helped me to reorganize the introduction and encouraged me in my efforts to place the notion of vehicles for solace in a larger, philosophical perspective. Thomas Kennedy, M.D., has been an invaluable source of support for the idea that psychiatric patients have legitimate transcendent needs and offered me a point of view about psychotherapy that was unique in its humanism. Paul Kay, M.D., Edward Casey, Ph.D., and Derek Miller, M.D., made specific suggestions that were helpful. Mrs. Gwin Cook provided patient and expert secretarial services and created an ideal office atmosphere. My wife, Kathy, was my best audience, listening to many drafts and helping me to make the manuscript as readable and down to earth as I could. Finally, to my patients, a very special thanks; without your trust and openness and, in some instances, remarkable courage, this book could not have been written.

SOLACE

Introduction

She had a severe demyelinating disease—a spinal type with brainstem involvement. There had been no significant remission in the last year. Her internist asked me to see her because of her depression. A thirty-two-year-old mother of two small children, she believed that her only hope was a "miracle." As we sat in her kitchen—she in a wheelchair and me next to her at the table—she told me tearfully of the pain of not being able to do her own housework and the terrible monotony of having to stay close to a toilet. She believed that her husband was both frightened and angry. He was often impatient and irritable and did not seem to want to talk with her. They had intercourse occasionally, but she found it too fatiguing. Her mother, with whom she had infrequent contact and who lived several hundred miles away, had not visited since before the onset of the illness several years ago.

Death was looking at me through her anguished facies. Dysarthria, hemiparesis, and neurogenic bladder were among the permanent disabilities. As we talked, I asked myself, What are potential vehicles for solace in her life? Her eagerness to talk with me and her religious views offered some possibilities that I began to pursue.

Later that afternoon, a fifty-eight-year-old lonely divorced father of four with a psychiatric disability entered my office declaring that he was at the "end of [his] rope." His daughter was in intensive care, "all smashed up" from an auto accident the night before. He recounted again the many dreadful things that had

3

happened to him and his children. With impotent rage he demanded an explanation for why "they" had it in for him. Who "they" were was not clear. Having seen the man weekly for only a few months, I could not be sure how seriously to regard his suicidal threats. There was a "burned-out" feel to him and his complaints. However, he had been physically violent with relatives and strangers in recent times.

His illness had begun in earnest shortly after his return from active duty in the South Pacific in World War II. He had been hospitalized at a veterans' hospital and had been given a diagnosis of paranoid schizophrenia. A dozen psychiatrists and every medication in the therapeutic armamentarium later, he was in my office demanding some explanation for why life was so painful, empty, and pointless. For the second time that day, I had to stretch hard to reach an idea of how life might come to have progressive meaning for a patient on the edge.

I scanned the understandings and hypotheses that are the essence of this book to see what therapeutic leverage I might apply. Finally, after he had demanded for the third time with growing impatience an answer to why he was being so mistreated in life, I suggested, "Maybe it's karmic." He looked puzzled and repeated, "Karmic?" I said that I certainly did not know for sure why his suffering was so extreme but that some serious students of suffering would claim that his collective misfortunes were karmic. The menacing anger temporarily aside, he asked me to explain further. After defining karma for him—the idea that what one does in one existence determines one's destiny in the next—I suggested that he himself may have done some grievous things in previous lives. Since the essence of his present hell was a feeling of helpless rage—that all kinds of devastatingly unjust things were happening to him and those closest to him—it is likely, if we accepted the karmic explanation, that he was a powerful destroyer in his last life. He interjected, "Do you mean that I might have killed without mercy?" I answered, "Yes—if we accept this explanation—you might have been a great warrior, or commanding general, or tyrant king who ruthlessly slaughtered his victims." After pondering this a bit he asked, "But why would these bad things happen to my daughters and to my son? The worst things that are happening to me now are happening to my children." I offered the idea of karmic "clusters"—that people with similar problems to work through in life tend to exist in close groups, as in families and friendships. I added that believers in karma state that suicide is the worst thing that a person can do to himself—that it may set one back centuries in development.

He stewed silently for several minutes and then asked, "Does karma work in this life?" I answered that, according to the theory, it does, and asked why he wanted to know. With a great effort he began a confession—the first time that he had admitted any guilt to me. He said: "Dr. Horton, I'm going to tell you something that I've never told anybody. The only guy who knows about it is an old man living up north of here who was my commanding officer in the Pacific. One day we were coming down off a mountaintop carrying wounded Japanese soldiers on litters. J.—the old guy—was in front, and we were carrying this Jap who kept begging for water. It was very steep, we were exhausted, and we could hear the gunfire further down the mountain. Finally, we just looked at each other—J. and me—and lifted the Jap over the side of the mountain. It was awful. He screamed and banged off the mountain all the way down. The others behind us looked at us and then took their litters and emptied them over the side of the mountain, too. We went back and got four or five more Japs and dumped them. This is why I ask, does karma work in this life?"

During the remainder of the hour he told me, without the flattened affect characteristic of his condition, how he felt about what he had done and why he thought he might have done it. One reason he gave was that when his unit landed on the beach they found a young blond marine standing with his arms tied around a tree. Before he had died his buttocks had been cut off. They found several other marines in the same condition, but for some reason the handsome blond youth had been imprinted on his memory and he could see him as though the event had occurred just recently rather than thirty-five years ago. Later in the day his unit had overtaken a group of Japanese soldiers and found the missing fleshy parts carefully preserved along with some tea. The Japanese were starving and had turned to cannibalism. My patient left the hour stating that he had changed his mind and would go to the hospital to see his daughter. It was a "test" of his courage, but if it would help in some small way he would give it a try.

Two years after a mastectomy, a depressed fifty-year-old woman lived in constant fear of metastases. She had many "scarey" dreams of disintegration, for example, dreams of "bits and pieces of material floating in deep, dark opaque water." However, she also had dreams of pretty, multicolored carpets. She associated them to the Orient, Persia, and finally to the idea of *magic carpets*. She recognized that in her dreams she was expressing a wish for the appearance of a soothing vehicle that would carry her to a larger meaning in life—and death.

A thirty-eight-year-old sales executive and father of four, who had nearly died three years earlier due to a vascular disorder and the resultant surgery, came to me for help with his alcoholism. He described repetitive, comforting dreams of sailboats—a metaphor for soothing change that I have encountered with many patients.

A socially isolated forty-three-year-old unmarried head librarian, who had been raised in an orphanage and could recall no instances of human closeness, stated: "My association with the church, however disconnected, has and does seem to offer some small amount of solace and comfort. The ceremonies, sacraments, and appeal of another and better world suggest an idea of belonging and caring, even though I only remotely feel that I can achieve what is promised or do receive any real succor from it as an institution."

So very much of my work as a psychiatrist revolves around the search for vehicles of solace. Whatever form the vehicles may take or symbolize—a religious idea, magic carpet, sailboat, or even the psychiatrist—they are the medium through which solace is experienced.

Not all vehicles that patients describe or seek are comforting. A forty-year-old man who had a stormy and unhappy business relationship with his father dreamed the following: He was a passenger on a DC-3—a twin-engine, propeller-driven aircraft that was, for many years, the mainstay of commercial aviation. He entered the cockpit and saw that the plane was flying too low and was about to crash into the skyscrapers of a modern city. In the next scene, he was standing next to the flaming crash. Emergency vehicles arrived, but they were too late. In his associations, the DC-3, a sturdy but outmoded aircraft, stood for his relationship with his elderly father, whose archaic ideas were ruining the business and holding him back. Shortly after this dream, the son terminated his business relationship with his father.

Moreover, some potential vehicles for solace disappoint. The psychiatrist who makes a person feel like the incarnation of an illness, or who underestimates or trivializes the problem with simplistic explanations, may give immediate or ultimate pain. The priest who behaves suppressively with people who cannot suppress, or the parent who habitually punishes without listening, are vehicles of disheartening pain. In *Winter Light*, Ingmar Bergman has a suicidal man ask his minister, "Why must we go on living?" The minister answers, "Because we must. We have a responsibility." The man left the church, went down to the river, and shot himself through the head with his shotgun.

Though the development of the ability to identify and create vehicles for solace is perhaps the most important challenge of becoming a psychiatrist, it is a missing dimension in psychiatric training. There were no courses in my medical, psychiatric, or psychoanalytic curricula that brought the existence of this dimension into focus. Anything that I learned in this matter was largely serendipitous—a spin-off of the humanity of my supervisors or of the conscious concern of an exceptional supervisor.

Indeed, the current psychiatric-psychoanalytic world view tends to deny the existence of consoling meaning in life, sickness, and death. A concomitant to the denial of a meaningful and transcending endpoint is the repudiation of the existence of the means. This is the main reason, I believe, that the larger implications of Winnicott's transitional object concept have been ignored or resisted.

This denial assumes three forms. The main psychoanalytic

manifestation is in the belief that *instincts*—sexual and aggressive—are the ultimate intrapersonal reality. The current *psychiatric* emphasis is on the physical sciences—behind every crooked thought is a crooked molecule. Less organically minded psychiatrists may get caught up in assessing psychopathology, diagnosis, even "social support systems," and simply not go to the heart of the matter, the patient's own system of self-soothing. There is also the "Ph.D.-ism" that afflicts both disciplines: meaning for the sake of meaning.* These points of view offer no elevating consolation for the distressing elements of the human condition unless intellectual elitism be its own consolation.

The failure of psychiatry to have developed a cogent endpoint perspective about human life not only makes the idea of vehicles for solace implausible and unimportant but also undermines the conception of sickness. A good example of this occurred when, as psychiatric residents, my colleagues and I were advised not to try to *cure* our patients. One of my first patients was silent with me for months, although I met with him five hours per week. His parents did not believe that their seventeen-year-old son was truly ill—little effort was made to convince them of this—and they took him out of the hospital. A few months later he put a gun in his mouth and gave final testimony to the "myth of mental illness."

Looking beyond the pristine scientific-intellectualistic world view of psychiatry to psychoanalysis specifically, we find little further enlightenment. Although good and evil are very important concepts to the overwhelming majority of the patients I treat, the serious mention of these notions in psychoanalytic circles is virtually taboo. Rizzuto (1979, p. 4) has said about the psychoanalytic study of religion that

> Freud himself—contradicting his own findings about the life-long importance of the father—insisted that people should not

* A good example of Ph.D.-ism is the well-funded attempt to apply "transformational grammar" in the clinical context (Leavy 1978). This unscientific exercise in linguistic circularity offers an "abstract physiology and genetics" (Chomsky 1978) to explain the essential aspects of the particularly human function of language.

need religion, called it a cultural neurosis, and set himself up as an example of those who could do without it. Intentionally or unintentionally, he gave the world several generations of psychoanalysts who, coming to him from all walks of life, dropped whatever religion they had at the doors of their institutes. If they refused to do so, they managed to dissociate their beliefs from their analytic training and practice, with the sad effect of having an important area of their own lives untouched by their training. If they dealt with religion during their own analysis, that was the beginning and end of it.

This book presents those vehicles for solace whose psychological significance transcends the pleasure principle and the repetition compulsion. In the distinctively human qualities with which they are invested, they go beyond mere instincts, narcissism, drives, motivation, sublimations, the sum of the defenses and language. They constitute the missing dimension in psychiatry.

Most everyone—mental health professional and layman alike—is familiar with the child's use of certain treasured possessions that serve as soothers. Linus, in the cartoon *Peanuts,* has come to represent an American stereotype of the child's relationship to the beloved blanket. The *Peanuts* cartoon is misleading in that, with the exception of Schroeder and his music, the other characters—Lucy, Sally, Pigpen, etc.—are not shown to be so related. The cartoon thus gives the impression that there is something exceptional, if not abnormal, about Linus's use of the blanket, whereas, in truth, the majority of normal children develop relationships to solacing objects at some time during their childhood.

The scientific observation of the ubiquity and normality of the child's relationship with such objects has been made a number of times since Winnicott's first reportage in 1953. The non-mental-health-professional, too, often takes these objects for granted as a normal accompaniment of growing up. This was brought home very clearly to me a number of years ago by the owner of an art store. While looking for a suitable picture for my waiting room, I came across one of a forlorn teddy bear. The bear was shown sitting on a barren window casing. A leafless tree could be seen silhouetted against a cloudy gray sky. I commented to the elderly proprietress that the poignancy of the teddy bear's abandonment would be appreciated by many of my child patients. She agreed, remarking, "Yes, they all have them you know." Unfortunately, she was not completely right—a small but clinically significant number of children are tragically unable to relate to any object that represents the good-mother relationship.

While there is general agreement among professionals that very young (i.e., pre-oedipal) children usually make healthy use of growth-facilitating soothers, the existence of such soothers at later stages of development has yet to be sufficiently recognized. In this book I shall show that the treasured soothers, or "transitional objects," of early childhood—exemplified by the blanket, stuffed animal, and favorite tune—are normally replaced by increasingly subtle and complex vehicles for growth and most especially for solace through a lifelong series of progressive psychological transformations.

A patient of mine helped bring the existence of this missing dimension into focus vis-à-vis her special problems. A forty-three-year-old disorganized, depressed, withdrawn, softspoken, divorced mother of one and fashion editor, she first came to me after having been "kicked out" of her previous therapy. She explained that she had developed sexual feelings toward her therapist and had begun to act seductively. Shortly before the termination of her treatment she had, with feigned inadvertence, touched her therapist's hand when he reached to open the door at the conclusion of a session. She recalled his angry panic: "Don't ever touch me again! You are my patient and you will always be a patient to me." This, of course, was just one in a series of increasingly intense provocations. The therapist acidly told me that she had a long-standing pattern of sexually taunting men and wished me "good luck."

To look at this dowdy, unhappy woman, it was virtually impossible to imagine her as a femme fatale. She clung feebly to life and required two brief hospitalizations to protect her from herself. This sense of her almost helpless, defeated vulnerability did not change much over the course of the next two years, during which time I saw her once or twice weekly in individual psychotherapy.

Her alcoholic husband had suicided five years earlier following their divorce. During their stormy marriage, she had had several extramarital affairs which she had made known to him. Eventually, he suffered a psychotic decompensation that terminated in suicide. Their seventeen-year-old daughter blamed her mother for her father's death and ran away. She became a prostitute and drug addict. The patient heard from her only when it was "bad news" and she needed money. The most highly charged emotional issue during the first two years of therapy was the loss of her daughter.

The patient's upbringing was brutal. Her father was an explosive alcoholic who often beat her with a razor strop and teased her sexually. She recalled her satisfaction, excitement, and unhappiness when he would arrive home late at night and vomit repeatedly from his drunkenness. The sound of his retching stimulated masturbation then and became a component of her present-day sexual fantasies.

As she became less depressed she grew more seductive both in and outside of the hour. When feeling better she was physically attractive and very sensitive to what men wanted. She had a knack for making a man believe that she was going to give him some forbidden, indescribably magical pleasure if he succumbed to her charms. After getting her way with him she rapidly wore him down, disgusted and smothered him with impossible cloying demands for emotional closeness. During her five years of treatment, many men, especially married men, came and went. Most of them silently disappeared, never to be heard from again. Others she excited, only to reject. An example of this was when she brought a weak, insecure man to her apartment on a number of occasions, sexually aroused him, and then threw him out. She took sadistic pleasure in his pathetic bewilderment and in his inability to free himself of her control over him.

Following a date with a schizophrenic man whom she found repulsive, she dreamed: "I was lying on my back in bed. I could see his ugly penis on the sheets between my legs. It was huge and bloody where it had been cut off." At the conclusion of what was to be her last date with this man, he drove her home drunkenly at over 100 miles per hour. She had "half wished" that they would crash and end it all. After hearing this I began to think of her as "my dangerous patient."

Her central masturbatory fantasy consisted of placing a man on an instrument of torture and slowly pulling him apart while bending his limbs until they broke. There were many variations on this theme that included flaying alive, smashing with an iron pipe, disemboweling, and other fiendish activities. A news magazine's pictorial section on torture in South America had greatly excited her, and she confided that she had wished, since she was a teenager, that she could have been a torturer in a Nazi concentration camp. While in Europe she had visited all of the medieval torture chambers and concentration camps she could find and had had numerous brief sexual encounters to relieve the tensions that built up on her journey.

Not being able to control men's lives sufficiently to literally tear them to pieces, she resorted to more subtle means. She could sense when a man was about to take masochistic pleasure in her humiliation of him and took measures to prevent this. Her victims did not seem to know what she was up to. She gave them only as much gratification as was necessary to cause them to fall into her hands.

There were many complicated transference issues, among which was her "torturing" of me with repeated references to her plan to kill herself if the therapy did not succeed. Eventually this expressed intent, along with her hostile seductiveness, remitted as she began to yearn for magical rescue by me. Perhaps the most important therapeutic activity to bring about this transformation was my inquiry into her relationships with objects, animate and inanimate, throughout the course of her life. Like most patients with severe personality disorders, she could not recall a single instance of soothing self-object merger. There was no history of relatedness to blankets, stuffed animals, imaginary companions, fairy tales, pets, heroes, religious figures, prayers, or any other personalized tangible or intangible.

The discussion of this patient and her therapy could take us in many interesting directions. However, there is just one facet that I wish to underscore: She had *almost* all of the psychological equipment she needed to function normally. Indeed, much of the time and in many areas of her life she did approximate normality. She had defenses, instincts, narcissism, drives, and motivations. She related symbiotically and transferentially and formed both dyads and triads. When not severely depressed she could daydream, fantasize, and play. Intellectually in the superior range and verbally adept, she was a keen observer and reporter of myriad realities.

Regarding her defenses, she even sublimated. Her job performance ratings were consistently good, and she usually took pleasure in her work. She was perceived by co-workers and me as having a good sense of humor—one that tended toward the dry and ironic. She could make sacrifices, as when she borrowed money to help her very unappreciative daughter out of legal trouble. In five years of weekly and twice-weekly psychotherapy I never saw her improperly groomed. Clearly, there were islands, if not archipelagoes, of healthy functioning. Virtually everything was hers—except the missing dimension.

The conceptualization of transitional relatedness—that is, soothing and growth-facilitating self-object merger—as a lifelong developmental process is in opposition to its usual restrictive definition as the attachment to the first not-me possession (American Psychoanalytic Association 1968, p. 93), the "infant's first plaything" (A. Freud 1963), or a mere "substitute object" for the mother (Bowlby 1969, p. 312). Perhaps Bowlby's represents the most limited and restrictive view of the role and importance of the transitional object:

A . . . parsimonious way of looking at the role of these inanimate objects is to regard them simply as objects towards
which certain components of attachment behavior come to be
directed or redirected because the "natural" object is unavailable. Instead of to the breast, non-nutritive sucking is directed
to a dummy; and instead of to mother's body, hair or clothing,
clinging is directed to a blanket or cuddly toy. The cognitive
status of such objects, it is reasonable to assume, is equivalent
at each stage of a child's development to that of his principal
attachment figure—at first something recognizable and expectable, and ultimately a figure persisting in time and space.
Since, pending more evidence, there is no reason to suppose
that the so-called transitional objects play any special role in a
child's development, cognitive or other, would a more appropriate term for them be simply "substitute objects"?

We must contrast such definitions with Winnicott's original
formulation (1953):

I am . . . studying the substance of illusion, that which is
allowed to the infant, and which in adult life is inherent in art
and religion. . . . I am not referring exactly to the little child's
Teddy Bear nor to the infant's first use of the fist [thumb,
fingers]. I am not specifically studying the first objects of
object-relationships. . . . I am concerned . . . with the intermediate area between the subjective and that which is objectively perceived. . . . It is assumed here that the task of
reality-acceptance is never completed, that no human being is
free from the strain of relating inner and outer reality, and that
relief from this strain is provided by an intermediate area of
experience which is not challenged [art, religion, etc.]. This
intermediate area is in direct continuity with the play area of
the small child who is "lost in play."

These and other quotes suggest that Winnicott *did* conceive the
transitional mode as a lifelong developmental process. However
he did not systematically explore and explicate the normal usage
of transitional objects by older children, adolescents, and adults,
nor was he specific about the psychological transformations that

must occur between the attachment to the teddy bear or blanket and sophisticated cultural experiences of many kinds. This book will fill in many of these gaps and provide a metapsychological explanation for the transitional phenomenon.

The first chapter is a "summary of pertinent literature" that will help to introduce the definitional chapter to follow and will serve as a backdrop for that exegesis.

The second chapter is definitional and is, in part, an examination and interpretation of Winnicott's original notions of the transitional object and phenomenon. His seminal contribution has led to many conflicting conceptions. An evidently charming and undogmatic man (see, e.g., *The Piggle* [Winnicott 1977]), he did not intend his papers to be the final word on transitional objects and remarked that there was a "wide-open clinical field awaiting exploration" (1971, p. xli). Perhaps the most important part of this chapter is the demonstration of a psychological continuity between child and adult transitional experience. The adult usage of certain objects, relationships, and experiences is a logical and culminating outgrowth of various earlier transitional object stages. The biggest challenge conceptually is to overcome the conviction that transitional relatedness is confined to the earliest stage or stages of the separation-individuation process and has no normal subsequent role.

The third chapter is a logical extension of the definitional chapter. In postulating the existence of a heretofore unrecognized developmental line, it is necessary to separate it clearly from overlapping and similar processes. Thus, transitional relatedness and the search for solacing vehicles is distinguished from pleasurable fantasy, transference, being in love, play, ego-ideal activities, sublimation, and narcissism and its transformations.

The fourth chapter is an elaboration of a particular facet of the second, transitional relatedness as a lifelong developmental process. The subphases of development are exemplified and discussed at length. Implicit in this chapter is a theory of object relations that may be schematized as follows:

Intrauterine
(oceanic) ——————————→ Primary ———————————→ Symbiotic
matrix   narcissism   relatedness

————————→ Transitional ——————————————→ Triadic relatedness
                object stage
                per se

Via transitional   Via transitional
relatedness   Post-oedipal   relatedness
——————————————————→ dyadic —————————————————→
                                 relatedness

                                 Via transitional
                                 relatedness

Higher-order object ——————————————————————→ Oceanic awareness
relations

    This very abbreviated scheme borrows from Freud's theory of object relations and Modell's (1968) interpretation of it (he "out-line[s]" [p. x] a "latent" [p. 7] theory of object relations discernible within Freudian theory) and his amendment, including the transitional object concept. It adds to Modell's conception a clearly healthy adult role for transitional relatedness, even unto the higher levels of human mental functioning.

    It is with respect to these "higher" levels of relatedness that special problems of exposition arise. I seek to demonstrate that the feelings and ideas associated with the quintessence of the transitional experience (i.e., the "maternal primary process presence") and its subsequent derivatives exist on many levels of organization from the most undifferentiated to the most highly differentiated forms. These "higher" forms are often associated with artistic and/or religious expressions. Recognizing that one man's religion may be another man's illusion, and that artistic taste is a highly individualistic affair, there are hazards in trying to portray these states. However, "No phenomenon can be completely grasped, in all its essence, until it has itself come to fullest actuality . . ." (Wagner 1892–93, vol. 2, p. 12). As might be inferred from the clinical examples given earlier, the recognition of vehicles for solace has great importance in the practice of psychiatry.

The fifth and last chapter explores the relationship between transitional relatedness and morality. One very useful clinical application of the transitional object concept for me has been in the understanding of severe character pathology. We (Horton, Louy, and Coppolillo, 1974; see also Horton 1976a, 1976b, 1976c, 1977) have shown that well-defined personality-disordered persons rarely exhibit transitional relatedness at any stage in life. The present work goes two steps beyond: (1) where the primary process presence of a soothing nurturing figure is not internalized, the capacity for transitional relatedness does not exist and severe character pathology results; (2) the existence of transitional states permits the coordination of cognitive and superego moral factors into a cohesive, well-functioning whole.

I suggest that the central moral problem of human existence is the conscious and/or unconscious wish to kill and to die. Two of my patients presented earlier (the "paranoid schizophrenic" man and the "psychopathic" woman), among many others, manifested such intense aggression that I was led to accept the hypothesis of a death instinct. Moreover, life itself—that is, the entire array of circumstances and forces outside the individual—sometimes shows an incomparable core viciousness, an apparent callous disregard of everything that humans feel, hope for, and expect. The woman with multiple sclerosis might have found death at the hands of a psychopathic murderer more tolerable than the tortures dealt her on the wheel of fortune. Whether the desire to kill ourselves or others is instinctual or cosmic in origin, our best refuge and convoy through life is the vehicle for solace.

Above all, I hope to interest the reader in the possibilities of the transitional phenomenon concept for a more general developmental theory. In this book, I try to indicate the main roads that must be traveled and the bridges that must be built in opening up this clinically essential and fascinating new frontier.

1 A Summary of Pertinent Literature

In recent years, the term "transitional," as in transitional object or transitional phenomenon, has come to have five main meanings attributed to it by various authors: (1) "transitional" from the mother to the larger world of animate and inanimate object relations; (2) transitional from the psychic or inner reality of wishes, desires, feelings, and ideas to the external world of inter-subjectively verifiable things—that is (using Winnicott's terms), from "me" to "not-me"; (3) transitional from one level of ego organization to another; (4) transitional from concrete to symbolic object relations; and (5) transitional in the phylogenetic sense.

Briefly, transitional in the sense of an expansion of object relationships from the symbiotic mother-child unit is the usual way in which the term has been employed in the child psychoanalytic literature. The attachment to the teddy bear or blanket is assumed to result from a "spill-over" (Mahler 1975) of attachment to the mother. Such objects may then substitute for the mother and soothe the child when ill, falling asleep, or engaging novel or conflictual circumstances.

The second meaning (from the psychic to the external world) pertains to Winnicott's statement that he was studying the "intermediate area of experience." Here, conscious appreciation of an object is the result of a relatively balanced blending of two tides of stimuli. One tide consists of the stimuli of wishes, feelings, instinctual yearnings, ideas, soothing fantasies, and the like provided from within and filtered through the person's ability for

18

creative, soothing illusion formation. The other tide is from the consensually validatable qualities of the object in the external world. Coppolillo (1976) exemplified the blending in the "intermediate area" of these two tides of stimuli:

> A teddy bear . . . can be appreciated for its size, its impish expression, the sparkle in its glass eye, and the softness of its fur. As it is brought into the transitional area of experience, to a child it can become much more. It becomes a willing recipient of loving hugs, or the abashed subject of a scolding for naughtiness, or even the victim of a well-placed kick in the rump. In a word, the child's inner states endow the inanimate teddy bear with lifelike qualities and roles. Yet, for all of the intensity of these contributions from the inner world, the child retains an appreciation of the teddy bear's objective qualities.

Either too much external reality, as with an objectively frightening event, or too much internal reality, as with a focused aggressive or sexual wish, may break the soothing spell of the transitional or intermediate area of experience.

The third meaning of transitional refers to the object's role in the evolving ego organization. Attachment to the object may either facilitate or interfere with psychological growth. In health, to experience an object in the transitional area is to feel maximally secure in the face of new and challenging internal and external realities. The emotional "refueling" (Mahler 1975) that accrues permits and encourages return to the novel or conflictual situation with renewed efforts at mastery. According to this perspective the transitional object is a catalyst for ego growth.

The fourth meaning of transitional—from concrete object to associative and, finally, symbolic object—is implicit in Winnicott's description of the infant's substitution of the soothing part-object for the mother (Winnicott 1971, p. 6).

The fifth, or evolutionary, meaning is not usually implied and is somewhat speculative but very intriguing. It has been suggested that the appearance of the florid ability for transitional relatedness in Cro-Magnon man is evidence of "a quantum jump of mind that established the adaptive superiority of Homo sapiens which eventually led to the extinction of the less intelligent Neanderthals"

(Modell 1968, p. 12). In this regard it is interesting to observe that certain nonhuman primates who, like Cro-Magnon man and unlike Neanderthal man, have survived the rigors of natural selection show transitional object relationships "identical with those seen in human infants" (Kollar 1972). However, it should be noted here that the transitional relatedness of chimpanzees, dogs, etc., does not develop into the complicated and subtle activity characteristic of human beings beyond the first few months of infancy.

Although various authors tend to emphasize one meaning or another, the several meanings of "transitional" are often implicit in their descriptions. For example, the "spill-over" of attachment to the mother onto inanimate objects may facilitate the infant's departure from the symbiotic orbit, thus permitting greater awareness of the external world. The "spill-over" definition is then compatible wtih "transitional" from inner to outer world. And since anything that leads to greater awareness of the external world may also result in increasing mastery, the third definition—"transitional" as from one level of ego functioning to another—is also appropriate. The various meanings are complementary and interlocking, and this fact proves to be one of the strengths inherent in Winnicott's concept.

Others have sought to extend Winnicott's creative and captivating formulation to a variety of phenomena and contexts far beyond the limits that many child psychoanalysts would find acceptable. Before summarizing some of these applications, it might be useful to consider remarks made by Kavka (1978) in his discussion of my paper on transitional relatedness as a developmental line. He traces Winnicott's concept back to Freud's "Formulations regarding the Two Principles of Mental Functioning." Kavka reminds us of the "psychic preserve analogous to the realm of fantasy in later development" (Freud 1911, p. 222)—the psychic activity that remains subordinated to the pleasure principle without interference from the reality principle. Kavka then quotes Ferenczi's 1913 paper, "Stages in the Development of the Sense of Reality," which includes the term "transitional," used in a sense that anticipates Winnicott's usage:

"The significant essay in which Freud displayed to us this fundamental fact of psychogenesis (i.e., repression) is confined to the sharp differentiation between the pleasure and the reality stages. Freud also concerned himself here with transitional states (in German, ÜBERGANGSZUSTÄNDEN) in which both principles of mental functioning coexist (phantasy, art, sexual life), but he leaves for the present unanswered the question whether the secondary form of mental activity from the primary takes place gradually or in a series of steps, and whether such stages of development are to be recognized, or their derivatives demonstrated, in the mental life of the normal or abnormal." [Kavka 1978, p. 182, quoting Ferenczi]

There is some evidence that Freud was insensitive to the psychological importance of the transitional mode per se. For example, in his article, "Screen Memories" (1899), he described a child's memory of damage to her dolls as an instance of the recall of relatively "indifferent" events. In fact, people very often recall the destruction of a transitional object with great affect and remember it as a very upsetting experience that proves not to be mere displacement.

However, there is, especially in the early Freud, another way of thinking about object relationships that anticipates in small part the definition I will give for transitional relatedness. In the "Project for a Scientific Psychology," he stated: "The aim and end of all thought-processes is . . . to bring about a state of identity . . ." (1895, p. 332). This was a point of view he reiterated many times and particularly with respect to the hallucination of gratification. Later, I shall suggest that the internalization of the soothing mother is a kind of learning analogous to imprinting and that relationships to transitional objects throughout life represent a search for that identity. In any case, there is little in classical psychoanalytic theory before Winnicott (1953) that may be used to explain the observations that have come to be considered "transitional" phenomena.

Following Modell's beginning efforts in 1961 to integrate transitional phenomena into an object relations theory, Stone (1966) was one of the first to apply the transitional object concept to the adult context: "For just as the child is assisted by the transitional object in his gradual progression to an object relationship which will provide what he (in an 'average expectable' sense) will require, the transitional but living analytic illusion in much more complex fashion, readies him for reasonably available real relationships, with a revised organization of internal images" (pp. 52–53).

Coppolillo (1967) and Kahne (1967) were among the earliest to pick up on and explore in depth the implications for adults of Winnicott's thesis. Coppolillo described how a psychotically depressed mother prevented a child from using transitional objects by "intrud[ing] and forc[ing] his attention back to her person." As a result he failed to develop the ability "to use substitute objects as deflectors or modulators of his wishes and drives."

Kahne called our attention to the much-neglected adult ramifications of Winnicott's formulation: "Winnicott sees in these events important implications for a concept of mind, play, scientific and artistic appreciation and creativity, imaginative living, religious feeling, and dreaming as well as in the domain of the pathological . . . and the origin and loss of affectionate feeling." Kahne described a twenty-four-year-old woman who, during the course of psychoanalysis, would defend against intolerable affects by "deliberately hum[ming], or sing[ing] to herself, or plac[ing] beads in her mouth"—behavior which he interpreted as "almost identical" to what Winnicott had described as transitional phenomena in young children. A twenty-three-year-old "schizophrenic" woman told him how she used dolls, jewelry, and other transitional objects into the present.

Since the observations of Stone, Coppolillo, and Kahne, several of us working independently have confirmed the idea that the therapist may become the adult patient's transitional object. Modell (1968), separating the transitional object relationship from the symbiotic and part-object relationships, emphasized the proclivity of schizophrenic and borderline schizophrenic persons to relate transitionally to others. ("The relationship of the borderline patient to his physician is analogous to that of a child to a blanket or teddy bear" [Modell 1963].) But he adds, significantly, "To some extent this mode of relating [the transitional mode] persists in all people and exists side by side with a more mature mode of object relationships where the object is clearly delimited from the subject" (p. 109). Modell sees the transitional mode as "a great psychologic divide with a progressive and a regressive side" and an essential ingredient in the artistic vision (Modell 1970).

Searles's (1975) formulation is similar to a part of Modell's: " . . . in order for any effective transference analysis to occur with any patient, whether neurotic, borderline, or psychotic, the analyst must have come to accept at least a transitional object degree—if not more deeply symbiotic degree—of relatedness with the particular transference image or percept which holds sway at that time in the analysis" (p. 202). Although he recognizes the importance of the patient's transitional object relationship to the therapist (and vice versa), he believes the transitional object phenomenon to be "tributary to, or consisting in various facets of the . . . more comprehensive realm of therapeutic symbiosis" (p. 147).

In potentially significant support of Modell's and Searles's observations is a recent study by Paul Arkema (1981). He discovered that forty-five patients admitted to a psychiatric hospital with a diagnosis of "borderline syndrome" exhibited a rigid, regressive, and often maladaptive transitional mode that included relationships with the therapist and significant others.

Ehrenberg (1976) describes the adult's *healthy* development of a transitional object relationship to the therapist and connects this with Winnicott's own observations (1971) of the importance of bringing patients to the point where such an experience is possible.

From my own work with patients who were depressed and suicidal (Horton 1973, 1974) and who utilized memories of the mystical experience as a transitional object, I recommended that the therapist actively seek to become the patient's transitional object, "thereby providing a reliably soothing, nurturant, reality oriented relationship." In contrast, it is necessary for the

therapist to assist the severely personality-disordered patient to
develop the ability for transitional relatedness—transitional relatedness directed to any object, since the core ego deficit is this
inability (Horton et al. 1974; Horton 1976a, 1976b, 1976c, 1977).
One implication of these findings is that the severely personality-
disordered individual, while not psychotic, is fundamentally more
disturbed than the schizophrenic. (See Kernberg [1970] for a
contrasting—and, in my opinion, mistaken—point of view.) Indeed, the therapist usually finds it easier to engage the schizophrenic patient in an emotional relationship than the psychopath.
It is the schizophrenic's ability to have experience in the transitional mode that makes him more psychologically accessible,
whereas the psychopath's inability to create and sustain a soothing illusion vis-à-vis the therapist may present an insurmountable
obstacle.

Davidson (1976) has described the differential appearance of
transitional objects according to the phase of treatment. (This is
reminiscent of Kahne's conclusion that transitional phenomena
may appear in psychoanalysis "under circumstances in which
there was a threat to the ego of separation from an important
contemporary object.") Some objects (such as a man's pipe, held
during sessions for the whole of the first year of therapy) may be
prominent during the early phase when the patient is anxious and
feeling a basic mistrust of the therapist. These "disappear when
the working alliance is established." The middle phase ushers in
the appearance of other objects that have greater cultural
significance and that signal the patient's strengthened efforts toward "individuation." An example is a middle-aged woman who,
after 280 hours, began to wear to the sessions jewelry that, as
cultural symbols of wealth, reassured her in the face of emerging
feelings of depression. The terminal phase may be accompanied
by the appearance of inanimate objects that represent the
establishment of the "internalized good object." Davidson gives
an example of a fiction writer who became preoccupied with a
special bathrobe that was associated with soothing memories of
her mother. Although Davidson does not suggest it, the patient
may also have been using her creative writings as transitional

objects: "I completed the final work of the analysis in a book of short stories and two full-length novels." In my own analytic work, I have found some tentative confirmation—too early to report in detail—of Davidson's idea of the evolution of transitional objects according to the phase of treatment.

In a provocative article, Searles (1976) has described instances in which the patient's symptoms and certain appurtenances in the analytic situation (e.g., tape recorder, the analyst's notes, psychotropic drugs, and the couch) were experienced as transitional objects by both patient and analyst. Regarding symptoms, Searles summarizes: "I surmise that many analysts, nowadays, are receptive to the idea that just as a patient's illness can come to be seen to be a kind of security blanket for the patient (personifying both the early mother and his own rudimentary ego), so the patient's illness can invest the analyst, in the course of the transference evolution, with the sense of a security blanket for him also. The result is that the eventual resolution of the patient's symptoms gives cause for feelings of loss, as well as of rejoicing, on the part of analyst as well as patient . . ." (p. 158). This sensitive insight has implications for analysis, "terminable and interminable": "It seems to me that any symptom on the patient's part which proves, over a long course of time in the analysis, highly resistant to further analysis is apt to have developed an unrecognized transitional-object function for the analyst as well as for the patient."

Natterson (1976) suggests, on the basis of the analysis of three men, that "it would appear possible that the analyst was experienced as the transitional object in [the] early phase." Then (in possible agreement with Davidson regarding the evolution of transitional objects according to the phase of treatment), it is observed that each of the patients came to experience part of the self as a transitional object. Natterson interpreted as follows: "At this point I told him that he had been his own security blanket, his own comforting doll. I said that one part of himself had this important attitude toward another part. . . ; this provided an illusory sense of comfort and security whenever he faced any pain or stress in life." Earlier, Solomon (1962) and Kafka (1969) had suggested that a "fixed idea" and the "body," respectively, can function as transitional objects.

Finally, I have claimed that the progressive use of transitional objects into adolescence and adulthood may culminate in oceanic or mystical experiences (Horton 1973, 1974). I offered the following explanation for a young woman's mystical states. This lengthy quotation is provided also to summarize many of the essential qualities of the adult transitional experience and to show the necessity of separating it from symbiosis.

> This patient's quest for the repetitive mystical state may be most completely understood, I believe, if it is seen as occurring in the "transitional" area of experience. Winnicott (1953) introduced the term "transitional phenomenon" to designate an "intermediate area of experience . . . symbolical of some part object, such as the breast . . . more important than the mother . . . a soother . . . a neutral area of experience which will not be challenged." Any thought, idea, or concept can function as a transitional object provided it is experienced in the "intermediate area" (Winnicott, 1953; Coppolillo, 1967). Winnicott (1953) said: "I am . . . studying the substance of *illusion*, that which is allowed to the infant, and which in adult life is inherent in art and religion . . ." (p. 90).
>
> My patient's recurrent mystical experiences are identical with more usual transitional phenomena in several ways: (1) Both experiences entail a blending of perceived inner and outer reality. (I am concerned here only with psychic reality. Commonly, those who have mystical states perceive part of the experience as originating from outside of themselves—"I was it. It was me.", etc.) (2) Both experiences have soothing functions and may be seen to be derivative of, or based on, the child's internalization of the mothering figure. (This is not meant to imply that the experience is *reducible* to the mother-child symbiosis.) (3) Neither experience is challengeable. Winnicott (1971, p. 96) states: "An essential part of my formulation of transitional phenomena is that we agree never to make the challenge to the baby, did you create this object or did you find it conveniently lying around?" In a parallel way, Salzman (1953) observes: "The conversion experience is hard to analyze. Most converts who come to therapy do so for problems other than their conversion. They are very resistant

to discussing their conversion experience; it is sheltered and protected . . ." (p. 185). (4) Both experiences come to be more important than the mother—an "almost inseparable part." In the case presented, the mystical awareness became a more reliable source of soothing than either mother or therapist. This was shown, for example, with respect to the latter during the closing stage of therapy when the patient returned to "meditation." This greater reliability in alleviating anxiety is a quality that distinguishes symbiotic from transitional relatedness. In the symbiotic relationship, the schizophrenic person strives to be, indeed, has no choice but to be *essential* to the object. As Lidz et al. state: "Perhaps the crux of the problem lies here, that the schizophrenic patient's primary concern is not with the development and defense of his own personality needs, but primarily with those of the mother . . ." (p. 63). The transitional relationship entails, in contrast, the exploitation of the object for purposes of maturation and self-soothing. Finally (5), both experiences exhibit maturational potential. Coppolillo (1967) hypothesizes: "Transitional objects and the transitional mode of experience are necessary elements in mediating the formation of those ego structures . . . which will permit socially appropriate and increasingly more mature forms of object relatedness" (p. 245). Similarly, the mystical experience may provide needed impetus for separation and individuation, as it did in the present case. The adolescent suffering from the pains of separation can be reassured and soothed much as is the baby by the special blanket, the child by the stuffed animal or myth, or the adult by a Bach Mass. Buttressed by the mystical experience, she is able to reconfront frightening internal and external realities and achieve a more adaptive integration. Such an experience may even serve as a suicide preventive. . . . [Horton 1974, pp. 372–74]*

Some, if not most, child psychoanalysts see the extension of the phrase "transitional object" to the disparate circumstances described above as a flabby and diffuse misapplication of the concept. Indeed, Coppolillo (1976), who is supportive of the larger Winnicottian implications of "transitional object" and who is not

* From P. C. Horton, "The Mystical Experience: Substance of an Illusion," *Journal of the American Psychoanalytic Association*, vol. 22, pp. 363–80, 1974. Reprinted by permission.

bound to a conservative analytic perspective, has nevertheless cautioned us about the "fuzzy" boundary lines surrounding its current usage and has pointed out the necessity for separating it from such phenomena as fantasy, transference, interest, and fascination. This caveat has been echoed more recently by London (1978), Hong (1978), and others. In a personal communication a noted psychoanalyst, who wishes to remain anonymous, stated: "Many analysts whom I respect not only reject [the idea of transitional relatedness as a developmental line] but are antagonistic to it. . . ." Such comments make it imperative to provide a clear and useful working definition of transitional relatedness and of the connected terms "object" and "phenomena."

Before turning to this task in the next chapter, I would like to bring you closer to the clinical material by citing several brief clinical vignettes from the literature. These examples are not comprehensive of the entire clinical field. However, they do, I hope, show something of how transitional relatedness comes to life in psychiatric evaluation and treatment.

CASE 1

[This elegantly presented case (Arkema 1981) exemplifies transitional object usage by a patient diagnosed "borderline syndrome."]

Ms. A, an 18-year-old coed, was admitted to the hospital after an overdose. She had participated in an unstructured group experience lasting several days; it included much talking, sharing sleeping quarters in a communal arrangement, and a sense of cohesiveness through a common cause. At the end of this event she experienced intense loneliness, emptiness, and anger. On admission, she complained of an inability to give enough to her new friends. In the hospital she exhibited regressive behavior and sought special consideration. She was hypersensitive, mistrustful, anxious, and despondent, and she denigrated the staff. Her anger was directed only at staff and not at other patients or visitors. She began to break windows and frequently cut herself, something she never had done before admission; this behavior continued until effective limits were set.

The patient perceived herself as a special child, her father's "special little girl," although she was always fearful of his anger and avoided him. She also felt isolated, envious of the only two childhood friends she could recall, and continuously lonely. She was angry with both of her parents for not knowing her fears as a child and was angry with her mother for working and not being home after school. Her parents, an engineer and a mathematician, often sent Ms. A to her grandparents for a weekend or when she was ill. The family placed a premium on manners and good behavior, on Ms. A's being "special or superior" to other children.

As a child she developed the habit of talking to her stuffed animals, who "understood" her hurt feelings. She felt better when she played with them. However, she said that immediately before admission, she found that talking with the stuffed animals no longer "worked" to soothe her. The animals no longer "sympathized" with her as she wished, and she felt they were hypersensitive, jealous, envious, suspicious, and resentful. It had been her practice since second grade to turn to her transitional objects for soothing whenever she was disappointed in a relationship, frustrated in fulfilling her emotional needs, dealing with separation issues, or angry with her care givers, especially her parents, for not satisfying her demands. She attempted to "squeeze warmth" from them, and when they failed to comfort her she became enraged and self-mutilative. She cut one of the animals to increasingly smaller pieces. She brought another animal to the therapist's office for protection. A breakdown in this mode of self soothing led to attacks on herself and to subsequent hospitalizations.*

CASE 2

[This patient is of particular interest not only because he used transitional objects "schizophrenically" but because employment

---

* From P. Arkema, "The Borderline Personality and Transitional Relatedness," *American Journal of Psychiatry*, vol. 138, pp. 172–77, 1981. Copyright 1981, the American Psychiatric Association. Reprinted by permission.

of them was a key to the proper diagnosis and understanding of his condition (Horton 1977).]

A thirty-four-year-old unemployed man was referred by his parents, with whom he still lived, for psychiatric treatment. He showed delusions of persecution, inappropriate and flattened affect, and other signs of chronic paranoid schizophrenia. However, he had been diagnosed as having an "antisocial personality disorder" as a teenager and had spent several years in a reformatory due to arsonous activities (possibly he was pre-schizophrenic when first evaluated). His schizophrenic condition had gone unrecognized for these many years, and he had even been dishonorably discharged from the Army as "unsuitable." He described a lifelong investment in transitional objects. His parents complained that he "hoarded" old things such as toys and stuffed animals. During the first interview he showed himself to be preoccupied with not only his own transitional objects but also those belonging to his teenaged sister, also schizophrenically disturbed. He stated that he had recently spent considerable time in an effort to find an exact duplicate of his sister's now worn-out "stuffed rabbit." He did not think she could manage without it. [P. 78]*

CASE 3

[This case, like case 2, shows the diagnostic utility of the transitional object concept (Horton 1977).]

An eighteen-year-old married fireman's assistant in the U.S. Navy with fifteen months of continuous duty sought psychiatric treatment for "depression" with "suicidal urges." He was refused treatment and found fit for full duty. Unable to accept this disposition, he entered a civilian psychiatric hospital while on leave. He was observed to be despondent, tearful, belligerent, and frequently "incoherent." He refused return to active duty and was transferred to a vererans' hospital. There

* From P. C. Horton, "Personality Disorder and Hard-to-Diagnose Schizophrenia," *Journal of Operational Psychiatry*, vol. 8, no. 2, pp. 70–81, 1977. Reprinted by permission of the Journal of Operational Psychiatry.

he was described as "extremely anxious, depressed, nervous though cooperative, and with very labile emotions." No "thought disorder, hallucinations nor delusions" were detected. It was felt by the evaluating psychiatrist that the patient was "unable to cope with the stresses of married life" and that this had precipitated his admission. He was transferred to the Naval Regional Medical Center (NRMC), Philadelphia, with a diagnosis of "inadequate personality disorder."

The patient evidenced signs of long-standing and "deeply ingrained maladaptive patterns of behavior" (DSM II, p. 41) compatible with and necessary for the diagnosis of personality disorder. Examples of his misbehavior were his expulsion from school in the tenth grade due to truancy, loss of driver's license for numerous moving violations, impulsive marriage, long-standing resentment of authority figures, absence of close friends, and isolation from peers dating back to early school years.

After one evaluation session, the admitting psychiatrist at the NRMC, Philadelphia, stated: "The patient is a shaky, tense young man with normal motor behavior. Speech shows no looseness of associations. Affect is appropriate and mood despondent. He describes active and current suicidal ideation and intent which he himself says is labile and changes from minute to minute. He is self-referential but exhibits no well-formed delusions." This psychiatrist also diagnosed the patient as having a personality disorder: "inadequate or emotionally unstable." Asked to explain his diagnosis, the admitting psychiatrist stated: "When I make the diagnosis, personality disorder, I do so with two considerations in mind: First, I regard the diagnosis as a prediction of behavior with a high degree of probability. In this case I felt that I could accurately predict that he would continue to beat his wife and literally and figuratively continue to tear off his uniform; also, that he would continue to show unstable but intense and appropriate affect focused on persons, organizations and institutions . . . , Secondly, I regard the diagnosis as a prediction of response to medication and psychotherapy: He will not respond. . . ."

Fortunately, the patient was fully evaluated as an inpatient over the course of several weeks at the NRMC, Philadelphia.

His behavior in individual sessions, on the ward, and on psychological testing (MMPI, Rorschach, WAIS, et al.) showed the presence of a developing schizophrenic disorder. His racing thoughts, ambivalence about his wife and the military, and emotional lability greatly improved with supportive psychotherapy and phenothiazine medication.

During the first interview with me the patient readily described transitional object usage as follows: "I used to have a green flexible, rubber frog that I took to bed with me when I was four or five years old. I often tied it to me with a string before going to sleep. One day my mother got angry and tore its legs off. Finally, she threw it away. I was pretty angry; she took something away that I really loved. Sometime after that I got a teddy bear. It had button eyes and was stuffed with cotton or something fuzzy.... One day my father and brother were monkeying around and hitting each other with it. They ripped it up but my mother sewed it together for me. I've still got the teddy bear around home someplace." [Pp. 77–78]*

CASE 4

[This depressed patient was regressively attached to tangible transitional objects even as a late adolescent, at which time she had her first mystical experience (Horton 1973). Following this transitional mystical experience she was able, over the course of a decade, to move ahead in her development, to complete her education, to marry, and to become a contributing, even moderately creative member of society.]

One of the youngest of many siblings, an early insecurity was evident in her thumbsucking and bedwetting, which continued until she was twelve years old. Stuffed animals, pets, a blanket, and other transitional objects were in prominent and excessive use until the patient was well into her late teens. She received additional transitional soothing from her early religious training: "I was brought up on what was a good dose of 'religion.' Church and Sunday school every Sunday, youth

* From P. C. Horton, "Personality Disorder and Hard-to-Diagnose Schizophrenia," *Journal of Operational Psychiatry*, vol. 8, no. 2, pp. 70–81, 1977. Reprinted by permission of the Journal of Operational Psychiatry.

group once a week, religious instruction classes during grade
school, Bible school in the summertime, Bible drills at
home—I even taught Sunday school during my high school
years, and I went to a Bible-centered college."

After enrolling at a distant college, she began de-
compensating "out of sheer loneliness." She sought refuge in
hallucinogens, which merely exacerbated her confusion and
sense of loneliness: "A major turning point came in my
life . . . when I mixed LSD-25 with alcohol. Bingo! I flipped out
fast; it was hellish. . . . I even went so far as to try to kill myself. The only truth I knew was that I was, indeed, in a hope-
less situation. Every other thought in my head was utterly
distorted and warped."

A psychiatrist was unable to help her, and other suicide at-
tempts followed. She said: "Just to give you an idea how utterly alone I was in the madness of my mind, even since re-
covering, I still can't find a human being who has or could feel
the pain, the fear, the hopelessness, nor aloneness, I felt
then."

It was then that she experienced her "conversion": "I remember looking around at the moment I understood I was
forgiven past, present, and future, and saying, 'Is that what it
is? Oh, is that what it is?' How did I feel? Like a huge knot
had been untied inside my head. For the first time in two
months, I slept soundly and peacefully; without fear; I was
filled with warmth and love for a living God." [P. 295]*

In a subsequent article (Horton 1974) I suggested that the mystical experience may represent a culmination—an end
product—of experience in the transitional mode.

CASE 5

[This case, like that of the woman described in the introduction, is
included to show something of the disastrous effects of not being
able to relate transitionally (Horton 1976).]

* Somewhat revised, from P. C. Horton, "The Mystical Experience as a
Suicide Preventitive," *American Journal of Psychiatry*, vol. 130, pp. 294–96,
1973. Copyright 1973, the American Psychiatric Association. Reprinted by permission.

A twenty-nine-year-old woman was first seen a few days
before the birth of her second child. Her obstetrician was at
his "wits' end" because of her chronic complaining. She had
already alienated her previous obstetrician and several other
physicians with perpetual carping about their failure to relieve
her many aches and pains. Her husband was also getting fed
up. The circumstances were reminiscent of the patient's early
life, when her parents told her, "No matter what you have
you're never satisfied." All potentially nurturing figures were
resented by the patient and were relegated to caretaker status.
Psychological testing verified the absence of psychotic or neurotic conflicts and confirmed a diagnosis of inadequate personality. She had no history of transitional relatedness.

The patient's nine-year-old daughter had, in contrast, both a
teddy bear and a "friend blanket." I asked her what ideas she
had about why her daughter had such attachments and she
had none. She stated:

> You see, my mother made me afraid of everything. I can
> remember her riding the school bus with me when I didn't
> want to go to kindergarten. When I was twelve or thirteen
> years old she was always after me about locking the doors
> at night and didn't want me to stay home alone. I think be-
> cause of my parents I never had many friends. I didn't like
> being alone but I hated crowds. Even today I don't like it if
> the neighbors bring their kids over. I can only take it for
> about ten minutes and then they start getting on my nerves.
> I can't keep up with what is going on when there are a lot of
> people around. I never felt secure. . . . The difference be-
> tween me and my daughter is that she can feel secure.
> . . . Her teddy bear makes her feel at home. It gives her a
> sense of routine. She doesn't feel strange when she has it
> with her. [P. 783]*

* From P. C. Horton, "Personality Disorder and Parietal Lobe Dysfunction,"
American Journal of Psychiatry, vol. 133, pp. 782–85, 1976. Copyright 1976, the
American Psychiatric Association. Reprinted by permission.

2 Transitional Relatedness Defined

Transitional relatedness is defined as the person's unique experience of an object, whether animate or inanimate, tangible or intangible, in a reliably soothing manner based on the object's associative or symbolic connection with an abiding, mainly maternal primary process presence. Characteristically and in health, this relationship facilitates engagement with novel, conflictual, even frightening circumstances and mediates or catalyzes psychological growth. To this must be added that, for most people, transitional relatedness is a developmental line—that is, a growth process and series of changes, often lifelong. It is influenced by experience and arises out of the interaction of elements provided through maturation and in response to the influences and attitudes of the environment.

This definition permits transitional relatedness to be distinguished from other forms of emotional relatedness to an object in which inner and outer elements intermingle and draw upon the whole of an individual's developmental past. It is the cohesion of these defining characteristics that separates transitional relatedness from pure learning, interest, fascination, pleasurable daydreaming, being in love, play, ego-ideal gratification, and mere sublimation. It also provides the basis for differentiating transitional from narcissistic phenomena.

An abbreviated version of this chapter was presented at the meeting of the International Psychoanalytic Congress in New York, 1979.

Let us begin by examining the elements—person, unique experience, object, etc.—of the definition. The part that pertains to it as a lifelong developmental line will receive some attention but deserves a chapter—the fourth—of its own. After parsing the definition, the psychological conditions with which transitional relatedness may be confused will be compared and contrasted.

"Person"

"Person," in the phrase "the person's unique experience," may refer to an individual of any age, ranging from a one-month-old infant to an elderly person on the deathbed. It is, of course, often difficult to be clear when an infant is first relating transitionally. Very briefly, Rudhe and Ekecrantz (1974) found that more than 10 percent of the children in their study showed transitional relatedness during the first two months of life. Winnicott mentioned a span of four to twelve months for the onset of transitional relatedness. Also, it will be shown in the fourth chapter that, for many normal people, transitional relatedness is as much an accompaniment of middle and late life as it is of childhood, and sometimes more.

"Unique experience"

The phrase "unique experience" refers to the fact that the individual brings special sensitivities and tendencies for varying modes of gratification to the encounter with the object. Describing this factor, we (Horton et al. 1974) said:

> The ability to personalize and to make an external object internally meaningful, we are suggesting, is a developmental milestone. It takes its origin, in part, from the time a child is able to imbue a toy or other concrete object with the life he feels stirring inside of himself. Even as he recognizes that the teddy bear is, indeed, cloth, stuffing and buttons, he suspends that aspect of reality just enough to permit himself to ascribe to the object those traits and qualities that he needs to see in himself at the moment. In this way, that teddy bear becomes his

teddy bear. Unique in the world and irreplaceable, it is that psychological area of the personal universe where the external physical reality of cloth, stuffing and buttons, becomes inseparably interwoven with the internal life of its owner. It acquires meanings that can be appreciated fully only by that owner. With further growth and development the object itself becomes less important in that almost any object or institution can be taken to a greater or lesser degree into the transitional area of experience. In that way, Beethoven's "Fourth Symphony" becomes infinitely more than a technically excellent arrangement of tones and rhythms. It becomes "my music" and with meanings for you and me that are probably different in shadings and intensities from those of any other listener.*

In the chapter on transitional relatedness as a lifelong developmental process, the great individual variation observed in the choice of objects will be abundantly exemplified.

"Object" (tangible, intangible, animate, inanimate)

"Object" has been partially defined in an earlier paper (Horton et al., 1974): "Here we speak of an object in the broadest sense (not only the child's teddy bear or blanket, or the adult's charm bracelet or good luck coin) and include nursery rhymes, songs, poems, religious figures, even unto Winnicott's 'ultimate stages of a human being's capacity for cultural experiences.' " It is the point of view of this book that any external thing, or person, or subjective content of experience, can function as a transitional object depending only on the way in which it is experienced. This is emphasized by the next phrases, "animate or inanimate, tangible or intangible."

"Object" is used to refer to both transitional objects and transitional phenomena. Winnicott (1953) distinguished (arbitrarily and unwisely, I think) between transitional objects and

---

* From P. C. Horton; J. Louy; and H. P. Coppolillo, "Personality Disorder and Transitional Relatedness," *Archives of General Psychiatry*, vol. 30, pp. 618–22, May 1974, Copyright 1974, American Medical Association. Reprinted by permission.

phenomena according to whether they were, respectively, tangible or intangible. A concrete thing, like a stuffed animal, was called an "object." An intangible thing, like a tune hummed to oneself, was called a "phenomenon." McDonald (1970) exemplified this distinction nicely: "... some children, who have experienced music from birth onward as an integral part of the loving motherly and fatherly caretaking environment might make use of music in a very particular way...; these children find in music their own special 'transitional phenomenon.' Some may even select from a musical repertory a special 'transitional tune' just as another child selects from his toys a special transitional toy."

However, object and phenomenon prove to be awkward locutions when defined this way since both have other and more generalized psychoanalytic and scientific meanings. For example, "object" in psychoanalytic parlance usually (but not always) refers to a person other than the self. Yet, judging by the literature, most child psychoanalysts reject the idea that a person can be a transitional object and insist on inanimacy as a criterion of transitional objecthood. This is in spite of the fact that Winnicott regarded animate things as potential transitional objects, for example, "I should mention that sometimes there is no transitional object except for the mother herself" (1971, p. 5).

Similarly, "phenomenon" is ambiguous in that it has a larger, generic meaning, referring to anything that can be scientifically described or appraised. It seems to me unnecessarily awkward to attempt to engage in discourse about transitional relatedness without using the word "object" to include people or the word "phenomenon" to refer to the facts, circumstances, or experiences—whatever they may be—that are to be described and appraised. To use "object" in the restrictive way that many child psychoanalysts and psychiatrists insist upon, or "phenomenon" in the way that Winnicott posited, is either to eliminate these terms from the psychoanalytic and scientific lexicon, respectively, when discussing transitional relatedness or to force the discussants to constantly qualify and redefine; for example, "I don't mean by transitional object only those objects that are inanimate but rather prefer to include living creatures or parts of them in the class of possible transitional objects," or "I wasn't using object in the sense of transitional object, as the child psychoanalyst might typically think of it, but rather as object in the classic psychoanalytic sense of object," etc. Or "When I used the word 'phenomenon' I didn't mean *transitional* phenomenon in the sense of something intangible and unmeasurable, but rather meant *this circumstance* (whatever it might be) that is apparent to the senses and that we are trying to describe," etc.

There is not, in my opinion, sufficient justification for us to continue to burden ourselves with paradox in the essential language of our discourse—"objects" that cannot include people and "phenomena" that are not apparent to the senses. Therefore, I propose that we use "object" to refer to *all* things—concrete or intangible, animate or inanimate, whole or part—toward which the transitional mode is directed. By this definition, any thought, idea, concept, or anything may be a transitional object if it is reliably and soothingly taken into the intermediate area of experience and fulfills the other definitional criteria.

The word "phenomenon" should retain its generic sense and give up the paradoxical connotation of intangible, unmeasurable, or invisible inner experience. Thus, I will be using the phrase "transitional phenomenon" to refer to the triad of the person, the transitional mode, and the object (whatever it may be) toward which the transitional mode is directed. I invite others to adopt this sensible and consistent convention.

A controversial issue, closely related to the distinction between transitional objects and phenomena, is the inclusion of animate and/or intangible foci for the transitional mode. There is a strong tendency in the literature to regard only those things that can be sucked, hugged, held, or stroked as legitimate contents of the transitional experience. Thus, Boniface and Graham (1979) erroneously conclude that only 16.4 percent of three-year-olds use "attachment objects." Their question to the children's mothers was: "A lot of children have a special cloth or rag, or something like that, that they take to bed with them or like to hold if they are tired or upset. Does X have anything like this . . . ?" There seems to be an uneasiness about relatedness to intangibles or even a belief that they are less important as attachment objects. (I prefer the phrase "relationship object" because it does not have the passive-dependent and unhealthy connotation of "attachment object." The children are not barnacles—they are relating, growing human beings.) The idea that attachment (or relationship) to intangibles and/or animate objects is less real or less important psychologically is often a reflection of a serious epistemological misconception.

Schafer (1976) has articulated, in attacking Hartmann's adaptation theory, a likely rationale for this misconception. He does not like the "anthropomorphism" that leads Hartmann to postulate what Schafer calls a hidden "mover of the mental apparatus" (p. 102), variously known as the "I," the "person," the "agent," or the "self." According to him, all such movers of the mental apparatus, hidden or otherwise, must be removed or excluded from analytic natural science conceptualizing. The basis for this is the belief that ideas such as "the self" are "abstract" and nonsubstantial." He says, "Customarily, we speak of thoughts, feelings, motives, traits, and suchlike *as though they had the properties of things,* such as extension, location and momentum, or the characteristics of people, such as tenacity, cunning and wilfulness" (p. 124, italics added). He regards our tendency to think of thoughts, feelings, and motives as "things" to be persisting "infantile or primary process modes of thought" (p. 125).

Astonishing as it may be, many of those who work with the inner states of others regard ideas, concepts, feelings, thoughts, fantasies, and other contents of subjective experience as somehow less real than "things" that they can hold in their hands. Therefore, when contemplating the possibility of intangibles serving as transitional objects (or even as "phenomena" in Winnicott's original sense) they may, if pressed, ask: "How can a thought or feeling be the target of a mode of experience if it has no extension, location, momentum or essence?" Put in this way there is only one possible answer.

I should like to shake the foundation of the above dogmatism by pursuing the line of inquiry further. If thoughts and feelings are not "things," that is, have no essence or substance, they must be *nothing!* Either thoughts and feelings have substance and exist, or they do not.

How many of us are willing to accept the logical conclusion of Schafer's argument: "Our thoughts and feelings—the contents of subjective experience—do not exist!" Most of us would probably acknowledge that the "feel" of a rock is different from the "feel" of a thought or emotional experience. But I doubt that many are willing to conclude from that that our thoughts and emotions have no essence or existence. Most of us accord existential status not only to conventionally palpable things, such as tables, chairs, and stones, but to other less tangible things such as molecules and atoms. Why wouldn't we do the same to the "things" that are more experientially immediate—indeed, the most immediate of all classes of things—that is, our inner states? Though the five senses are in abeyance in them, these private awarenesses are, in James's words, "absolutely sensational in their epistemological quality" (1902, p. 415).

Perhaps one rejects the idea of the existence of inner states as objects of the transitional experience on practical grounds (i.e., that the empirical scientist must be able to see objects as external to the self): If they are inside of another person one cannot be sure that they are reliably soothing objects in the same way as the teddy bear or blanket. The main objection I have to this methodological stricture is that it smacks of the "drunkard's search" (Kaplan 1964): "There is a story of a drunkard searching under a street lamp for his house key, which he had dropped some distance away. Asked why he didn't look where he had dropped it, he replied, 'It's lighter here!' "

Therefore, the "object" in transitional object is being defined in its broadest, most conceptually challenging, and simultaneously most valid sense to include poems, prayers, tunes, nursery rhymes, imaginary companions, and many other personalized intangibles.

"Reliably soothing manner"

The phrase "reliably soothing manner" is also controversial but necessary if the net of determinants for what is transitional is not to be spread too widely and the definitional boundaries are not to become too fuzzy. It is a fact of observation that the blanket or teddy bear (or any other transitional object) does more to *soothe* the child than anything else. Confusion may occur when the object has other or multiple nonsoothing functions. In addition to being a soother, an object may serve as a toy, tool, souvenir, work of art, ornament, weapon, source of information or amusement, and many other things. Sometimes the distinctions are easy to make: If the object's primary impact is to amuse, we call it a toy; if to sexually stimulate, a fetish (Greenacre 1969); if to provide warmth, a blanket; if to frighten, a phobic object; if to remind one of a lost attachment, a linking object, etc. What is definitionally important is that when the object is being used transitionally it is a soother.

"Circumstances that affect an object's soothing function"

The fact that an object may be used for purposes other than soothing does not mean that it is not, cannot be, or has not been a transitional object.

An alteration in the object itself

A change in the object may make it temporarily or permanently unsuitable for use as a transitional object: washing a special blanket may eliminate the required smell; tearing an eye off a stuffed animal or disfiguring a doll may render it useless until repaired; a spouse's increasing independence may impair his or her reliability as a soother and result in a breakdown of that function. An example of the temporary loss of soothing function due to damage of the object is the following:

> A mother recently presented her now grown daughter with a letter the former had sent to the latter's grandmother in 1947 describing her three-and-one-half-year-old daughter's reaction to having her favorite doll repaired. The doll had been damaged by a sibling. The letter read: "Bob went to the Chamber of Commerce meeting last night and was made Chairman of the Safety Committee. He was very pleased about that be-

cause he has some very definite ideas about some of the safety rules in this town. He got home about 9:30 and we spent the rest of the time from then until 12:00 vulcanizing a patch on Kathy's big doll. She hasn't played with it for at least six months. So after we got it all patched and cleaned up I dressed it and set it in her doll bed so she would see it first thing in the morning. Well, she had to go to the bathroom about four o'clock in the morning so I turned on the bathroom light and told her to come. I went to her door to see if she was coming and she got out of bed and came to the door. Then she stopped quick with a funny look on her face and whirled around and ran back to her doll bed to take another look (it was fairly dark). She let out the happiest cry and said 'Oh, my daddy fixed you didn't he!' Honestly, it was better than Christmas. I finally got her to go to the bathroom and all the time she talked a blue streak to the doll and to me. Then she took the doll and very lovingly laid it on the bed and climbed in beside it. I stood in the hall for awhile to see what she would do and she lay there whispering to the doll, too excited to go to sleep. When I got up this morning she was sound asleep with both arms around the doll."

Following repair of the doll it again became her favorite soother for several years.

The above example also illustrates the idea that a change in the object not produced by its owner violates the stricture that the object is creatively chosen, in all of its essentials, by the owner and the owner alone (Winnicott 1953).

An alteration in external conditions

External conditions may affect interpretation of a transitional object's features. For example, a forty-five-year-old man who had been abandoned by his parents at age four recalled his teddy bear as follows: "I liked to nap with my teddy during the day. But I never took it to bed with me at night. I was afraid of its eyes staring at me in the dark or something bad happening." The stimulus deprivation of darkness, coupled with what he felt to be an unsupportive, hostile environment, permitted the angry, dangerous, sexually monstrous determinants of bear choice to become too conscious. In the dark he was unable to appreciate the bear for its impish expression and the gentle sparkle in its eyes.

Internal psychological changes

Growth

In the typical case, a child outgrows a particular soother and relegates it to the dresser drawer, closet shelf, or attic. Rarely, it is thrown away. It is often recalled for brief periods of use well into latency. It is usually not forgotten or repressed but is simply replaced by more age-appropriate objects. Adults too may outgrow transitional objects. For example, a young man could not sleep without his special pillow until he married. His wife then became his primary soother and the pillow was given up.

Onset of emotional disturbance

A historically interesting example may be taken from Freud's Little Hans (1913). The competitor with the horse for the role of Little Hans's bugbear was the giraffe. A picture of a giraffe hung over Little Hans's bed (p. 39). The giraffe had been his bedtime companion and amusement (p. 33)—a transitional object helping him to fall asleep—before becoming a phobic object.

Resolution of illness

Conversely, the resolution of an illness may lead to the exchange of one transitional object for another. An example is that of a three-year-old boy with a dog phobia who rejected one stuffed animal after another offered to him at a toy store. About the stuffed dogs he made statements such as, "I don't want that one—its eyes are too scarey!" and "I don't like it—its face is mean!" He settled on a small stuffed kitty. He used the kitty for about a year and then replaced it with a big stuffed dog, even bigger than the dog his brother used. This occurred only after the remission of his dog phobia.

"Mature soothing"

The discussion of soothing has so far emphasized the child's experience. Of course, for infants and small children the definition of "soothing" is largely behavioral and empathic. The baby clutching the special blanket to help him fall asleep is "soothed" by the presence of his object. Conversely, sudden deprivation of the blanket—as occurs when unwise parents try to force the child to give up the transitional object—results in obviously anxious, restless, and disconsolate behavior with pleas for its speedy return.

What precisely is "soothing," or the more adult "solace," when we move beyond the earliest developmental stages into adolescence and adulthood? How is transitional soothing to be distinguished from instinctual pleasures? And more complexly, how is transitional soothing to be separated from aim-inhibited gratifications such as esthetic pleasure?

In order to begin to answer the above questions, I must discuss the meaning of "maternal primary process presence"—the crucial explanatory link between the transitional relatedness of infancy and old age. Therefore, I will save "associative and symbolic connection" until the discussion of soothing and its related psychological substructure, the maternal primary process presence, is completed.

"The mainly maternal primary process presence" (and its relationship to transitional soothing)

Primary process presences are those psychological internalizations of other people, or aspects of them, that were formed during early childhood and that have become unconscious except under special circumstances. Schafer (1968) orients us to the phenomenology of a frequently experienced primary process presence: "In everyday life, primary process presences are commonly experienced in social situations in which one feels the 'presence' in the group of another person with whom one is not directly engaged at that moment. Often that 'presence' can be felt almost physically, and, typically, it is not simply or clearly experienced as inside oneself or as merged with oneself'' (p. 122). He adds that the conditions for the coming about of such an experience are a ''strong wishful response to the object,'' a ''fantasy,'' and an ''altered state of consciousness.''

Other primary process presences do not depend on the actual, current presence of the object. The following exemplifies a soothing maternal primary process presence: ''When Breton fishermen were out at night in stormy weather in the Atlantic they used to see a vision: an old woman sitting in the bow of the boat singing lullabies to them. They were not afraid of her because they knew that she was the 'cradle woman,' the old nurse who used to rock them to sleep when they were small and who had come to rock them to rest in the tossing boat'' (quoted from Heiman [1976]).

Some presences are not even clearly related to an object past or present: '' 'On two other occasions in my life I have had precisely the same ''horrible sensation.'' Once it lasted a full quarter of an hour. In all three instances the certainty that there in outward space there stood *something* was indescribably *stronger* than the ordinary certainty of companionship when we are in the close presence of ordinary living people. The something seemed close to me, and intensely more real than any ordinary perception. Although I felt it to be like unto myself . . . I didn't recognize it as any individual being or person' '' (James 1902, p. 60).

Others are more ambiguous in origin: '' 'There was not a mere consciousness of something there, but fused in the central happiness of it, a startling awareness of some ineffable good. Not vague either, not like the emotional effect of some poem, or scene, or blossom, or music, but the sure knowledge of the close presence of a sort of mighty person, and after it went, the memory persisted as the one perception of reality. Everything else might be a dream, but not that' '' (James 1902, p. 60).

With respect to maternal primary process presences specifically, some are soothing and others painful. A person who usually experiences a soothing presence may occasionally become aware of a painful or frightening internalization of the pregenital mother. Some unfortunate people have mainly painful internalizations of a not-good-enough mother. For example, patients (usually women, occasionally men) who have intense spider phobias, nightmares, and hallucinations hide the negative maternal primary process presence behind a thin symbolic disguise. (See Ingmar Bergman's film, *Through a Glass Darkly*, for a gripping portrayal of the internalized spider mother and its psychologically devastating effects.)

There are many other possible symbols of the painful maternal primary process presence. For example, a woman had recurrent nightmares of being alone in the dark and on a desert while a siren screeched unremittingly—a symbol of the feared and hated pregenital mother. Also to be considered are various mixtures of the soothing and painful primary process presences that a great many people exhibit. However, when a person is experiencing the depriving, injurious maternal primary process presence, he or she is not at that moment capable of experience in the transitional mode.

A partial explanation for the origin of the soothing maternal primary process presence is the following: An "omnipotent sufficiency" characterizes the earliest months of life and is "maintained, for a time, by the close 'symbiotic' relationship with the mother" (Loewald 1962, p. 495). An intense, richly gratifying symbiosis consolidates what is first a conscious and later an unconscious and derivative sense of fusion with the nurturant breast-mother. This abiding sense may, after weaning, become conscious from time to time as a "primary process presence." This "continued internal existence" (Schafer 1968, p. 77), this primary process or "felt presence . . . serves the interest of a maintained libidinal tie to the mother" (p. 77). The " 'good' mother 'presence,' the primary-process idea of her is experienced . . . even while the actual mother is 'known' to be absent or involved in other matters" (p. 77). This is the abiding, usually lifelong psychological substructure that permits the child and adult to feel safely fused or merged with a protective and nurturant figure or life force. As Jacobson (1964, p. 41) points out, this sense of fusion—this soothing illusion—is normally conscious until about three years of age, after which it is usually relegated to the unconscious.

The above observations notwithstanding, we may still ask, What makes the maternal presence soothing, that is, what are the special qualities that endure and that constitute the driving force behind transitional activities throughout life? I would suggest that to the extent that the maternal primary process presence is connected with the latent oceanic experience it is soothing. The mother that stands—both developmentally and experientially—next to the unconscious oceanic state is, if we have her, the perfect woman of our dreams, visions, and yearnings. She is, as it were, the stuff of the Flying Dutchman's eternal vision and quest. She is the great rescuer, redeemer, and deliverer. She represents the "tie so subtle that it is at first invisible even to those whom it unites" (Kobbé 1972, p. 247). She is the Valkyr who carries the slain warrior to Valhalla, the selfless Isolde, the ultimate nurturant earth-mother. She, like Scheherazade, can at least neutralize the destructive beast within all of us, if not transform it, into its transcending opposite.

This paradisal mother may be an end in herself. (I think of Guido floundering helplessly in the fountain as he worshipfully pursued his goddess in Fellini's *La Dolce Vita*.) This is because the ultimate goal, the complete oceanic awareness, is too deeply repressed for most of us to make it an aim of life. Moreover, the soothing maternal primary process presence embodies some of the elements of the oceanic state—it is the first important object-related psychological structure to emerge, the awareness of which may be sufficiently solacing.

It is probably clear by now that the soothing that results from transitional activities is not to be equated with mere instinctual pleasures or even with "sublimated" ones. Since the penultimate goal of transitional relatedness is the reexperiencing of the maternal primary process presence, and the ultimate goal is the achievement of the oceanic state itself ("the wide ocean of eternal beauty," in Platonic terms), transitional solace is qualitatively separable from and more psychologically basic than all other pleasures and joys.

It is difficult to be precise and to engender clinical conviction about the qualities of the oceanic state that support the soothing maternal primary process presence. For most of us the oceanic or mystical state is on the edges of experience. However, I will try to give at least some approximate notion of what I mean by "oceanic" or "mystical." Let us turn to literature, and first of all to Hemingway's *For Whom the Bell Tolls*. In the scenes to follow, Robert Jordan is making love to Maria, after which they are questioned by the strange earth-mother, Pilar:

> ... For him it was a dark passage which led to nowhere, then to nowhere, then again to nowhere, once again to nowhere, always and forever to nowhere, heavy on the elbows in the earth to nowhere, dark, never any end to nowhere, hung on all time always to unknowing nowhere, this time and again for always to nowhere, now not to borne once again always and to nowhere, now beyond all bearing up, up, up into nowhere, suddenly, scaldingly, holdingly all nowhere gone and time absolutely still *and they were both there, time having stopped and he felt the earth move out and away from under them....*
> "Maria," Pilar said, "Now and of thy own volition. You hear me? Anything at all."
> "No," the girl said softly. "No and no."
> "Now you will tell me," Pilar told her. "Anything at all. You will see. Now you will tell me."
> "The earth moved," Maria said, not looking at the woman. "Truly. It was a thing I cannot tell thee."
> "So," Pilar said and her voice was warm and friendly and there was no compulsion in it. But Robert Jordan noticed there were small drops of perspiration on her forehead and her lips. "So there was that. So that was it."
> "It is true," Maria said and bit her lip.
> "Of course it is true," Pilar said kindly. "But do not tell it to your own people for they never will believe you...."

"Three times," said Pilar. "Now you've had one."
"Only three times?"
"For most people, never," Pilar told her. [Pp. 159–75,
italics added]

The second example is taken from Romain Rolland's brilliant
Nobel Prize–winning *Jean-Christophe* (1913). In this scene an
elderly musical genius—probably modeled on the life and writings
of Richard Wagner—is dying:

Then bells rang tranquilly. The sparrows at the window
chirped to remind him of the hour when he was wont to give
the breakfast crumbs. . . . In his dream Christophe saw the little room of his childhood. . . . The bells. Now it is dawn! The
lovely waves of sound fill the light air. They come from far
away, from the villages down yonder. . . . Once more Christophe stood gazing down from the staircase window. All his
life flowed before his eyes, like the Rhine, All his life, all his
lives, Louisa, Gottfried, Oliver, Sabine. . . .
    "Mother, lovers, friends. . . . What are these names? . . .
Love. . . . Where are you? Where are you, my souls? I know
that you are there, and I cannot take you."
    "We are with thee. Peace, O beloved!"
    "I will not lose you ever more. I have sought you so long!"
    "Be not anxious. We shall never leave thee more."
    "Alas! The stream is bearing me on!"
    "The river that bears thee on, bears us with thee."
    "Whither are we going?"
    "To the place where we shall be united once more."
    "Will it be soon?"
    "Look."
    And Christophe, making a supreme effort to raise his
head—(God! How heavy it was!)—saw the river overflowing
its banks, covering the fields, moving on, august, slow, almost
still. And, like a flash of steel, on the edge of the horizon there
seemed to be speeding towards him a line of silver streams,
quivering in the sunlight. The roar of the ocean. . . . And his
heart sank, and he asked:
    "Is it He?"
And the voices of his loved ones replied:

"It is He!"
And his brain dying, said to itself:
"The gates are opened. . . . That is the chord I was seeking!. . . But it is not the end! There are new spaces!. . . We will
go on, to-morrow."
O joy, the joy of seeing self vanish into the sovereign peace
of God, whom all his life he had so striven to serve!. . .
"Lord, are Thou not displeased with Thy servant? I have
done so little. I could do no more. . . . I have struggled, I have
suffered, I have erred, I have created. Let me draw breath in
Thy Father's arms. Some day I shall be born again for a new
fight."
And the murmuring of the river and the roaring of the sea
sang with him:
"Thou shalt be born again. Rest. Now all is one heart. The
smile of the night and the day entwined. Harmony, the august
marriage of love and hate. I will sing the God of the two
mighty wings. Hosanna to life! Hosanna to death!"

Shortly before this scene the dying composer had given a beautiful example of primary process presences: "How good it is to
think, at the end of life that I have never been alone even in my
greatest loneliness!. . . Souls that I have met on the way,
brothers, who for a moment have held out their hands to me,
*mysterious spirits sprung from my mind, living and dead—all
living.*—O all that I have loved, all that I have created! *Ye surround me with your warm embrace,* ye watch over me. I hear the
music of your voices. Blessed be destiny, that has given you to
me! I am rich, I am rich. . . . My heart is full!. . ." (italics added).

The oceanic experience must be distinguished from experiences connected with the nirvana principle and its modification in the pleasure principle. Freud—who could not hear the
music (Freud 1927, p. 65)—described nirvana as a return to the
inorganic state, that is, to a condition of absolute nothingness
viewed from the perspective of everything that human beings
cherish. In contrast, the onset of the oceanic state is accompanied
by a reaffirmation of one's connectedness to essential others—
especially those soothing, loving, all-embracing, should I say
maternal, others.

The third example of the intimate relationship between the maternal primary process presence and the oceanic or mystical state comes from *The Confessions of St. Augustine*. Augustine was with his mother when his conversion began:

> Now the day was approaching on which she was to leave this life . . . and so it happened that she and I were standing alone . . . with the mouth of our heart we panted for the heavenly streams of your fountain, the fountain of life. . . . And still we went upward, meditating and speaking and looking with wonder at your works, and we came to our own souls, and we went beyond our souls to reach that region of never failing plenty . . . [Pp. 200–201]

Finally, we may contemplate Saul Bellow's linking of the maternal presence—taking "mother earth" as a representative of the maternal primary process presence—to the oceanic, mystical, or perhaps, in this instance, cosmic state:

> The air, the very air, is thought-nourishing in Jerusalem, the sages themselves said so. I am prepared to believe it. I know that it must have special properties. The delicacy of the light also affects me. I look downward toward the Dead Sea, over broken rocks and small houses with bulbous roofs. The color of these is that of the ground itself, and on this strange deadness the melting air presses with an almost human weight. Something intelligible, something metaphysical is communicated by these colors. The universe interprets itself before your eyes in the openness of the rock-jumbled valley ending in dead water. Elsewhere you die and disintegrate. *Here you die and mingle*. [P. 12, italics added]

In this quotation and elsewhere in *To Jerusalem and Back*, we hear the recurring themes of mother earth, loving and sensuous reunion, soothing nurturance, transcendent illusion, and unchangeable specialness in concert in the intermediate area between the mature author and his object of devotion—all qualities of the transitional experience.

We will return to the issue of the underlying multipotential oceanic state in the chapters to follow.

The qualifier "mainly," in the phrase "mainly maternal primary process presence," is included to take into account the possibility that others, such as the father, a grandparent, or an older sibling, may provide significant auxiliary internalizable soothing or "mothering." Thus, the adjective "maternal" is used in a larger sense than merely "female parent." Yet the quality and depth of the internalized soother is undoubtedly predicated on the presence of a well-defined, reliable, and empathic special One. (Studies on children hospitalized during the first year of life lend strong support to this conclusion [see Provence and Lipton 1962; Spitz 1965].)

An interesting ramification of the idea that a maternal primary process presence underlies transitional relatedness is the possibility that object constancy may arise in some infants during the first month or two of life. In fact, there is an apparent, perhaps real, conflict between observations of transitional relatedness during the first two months of life and various opinions of when the infant is first able to develop a stable memory image or mental representation of the mother. For example, Piaget, using test toys, concluded that eighteen months is the time when evocative memory becomes possible. Since the five-to-eight-months-old infant will not attempt to find a toy placed behind a screen before his eyes, it is concluded by Piagetians that the infant has no ability for forming stable mental representations of the object. In contrast, Spitz, using the development of stranger anxiety as a criterion, claimed that the ability to establish a stable, evocative image of the mother develops as early as eight months of age.

This is a very complicated and moot issue among the various psychologies the nuances of which have been reviewed by Fraiberg and her colleagues (1969). I shall not discuss it further here, other than to point out that the existence of transitional object attachment at one or two months of age suggests either: (1) that our concepts of the meaning of very early transitional relatedness, that is, its representing a "spill-over" of attachment to the mother, must be revised; or (2) that the age at which stable, evocative maternal imaging—conscious or otherwise—can occur is much earlier than even Spitz's estimate. At the least, a semantic problem exists: The phrase "transitional object" connotes the prior existence of a relatively stable mental representation of the mother on the basis of which a "transitional" or "spill-over" can occur. To deny that the two- or three-month-old can form an evocative maternal image compels us to conclude that this early "transitional" behavior is not really transitional at all—that it does not have the same object-related basis that characterizes later transitional relatedness.

We would then be left with the question of what this early "transitional" behavior represents. Perhaps it is a function of the infant's still diffuse and indiscriminate capacity for relatedness. In possible support of this is Rudhe and Ekecrantz's observation that children with *multiple* relationships (to such things as sounds, movements, and especially soft toys) exhibited transitional behavior earlier than others. Early multiple attachment could be interpreted as evidence of an undifferentiated capacity for relatedness that is, as yet, unconnected with an image of the soothing mother.

On the other hand, we might wonder about the attachment selectivity that even those with multiple objects show. After all, they do not become attached to every available soft object; their attachments are not really indiscriminate. Moreover, my studies of later versions of transitional relatedness at all stages of life lead me to emphasize the role of evocative maternal imaging: the invariable existence of a maternal primary process presence as the source of all postinfancy transitional relatedness should at least make us consider the possibility that even the one- or two-month-old infant may have formed such an image.

The conflict between my position and that (e.g., Piaget's) which posits the necessity of much-later-developing "cognitive" factors in the genesis of an evocative image of the object cannot, in any way that I can see at this time, be resolved by a "crucial" experiment. The observation of the development of an anaclitic depression in a three-month-old infant (Gaensbauer 1980) certainly lends support to my idea that specific relatedness to the mother may occur much earlier than is generally supposed. Ten days after being transferred to a foster home, a three-month-old infant was brought together with her mother for a brief visit: "An onlooker noted that Jenny immediately recognized her mother's face and 'lit up like a Christmas tree' with broad smiling and excited activity." After three weeks of separation the child was clearly depressed: "She seemed apathetic and disinterested in her environment and could not be engaged in play. Smiling was almost absent. She was easily upset and fussed when she was overstimulated."

The above connects with Kohut's hypothesis (1977, pp. 98–100): " . . . we may well discover, as we investigate early states of infancy with more and more refined psychological means, that a rudimentary self is already present very early in life—the human environment reacts to even the smallest baby as if it had already formed such a self. . . ; he is, from the beginning, fused via mutual empathy with an environment that does experience him as already possessing a self." Kohut's observation raises the interesting possibility that researchers and theoreticians do not adultopomorphize enough when attempting to gauge the inner state of the infant, especially the latter's object relatedness.

I should like to refer briefly to an explanatory framework that makes my postulation of the formation of a stable mental representation of the mother during the first six months of life—admittedly, well in advance of the development of many ego functions—plausible. I do this to show that there is at least one way in which my contention might find theoretical justification. Therefore, the following is not offered as proof but rather as an example of a way of thinking about these apparently irreconcilable differences. It comes to this: Human infants, like other species of animal, may be capable of two types of learning. The first type is the one we are all familiar with and is characteristic of more fully developed ego functions (i.e., associative learning). The second type has been demonstrated ethologically and is called "imprinting." A well-known example of imprinting may be taken from Lorenz's experiments. Goslings, separated from their mothers during the first few days of life, learned to follow Lorenz as though he were their mother after which "the human-imprinted gosling . . . unequivocally refuse[d] to follow a goose instead of a human" (Lorenz 1965, p. 37). This observation fits nicely with Freud's contention that all perception is a "search for identity" and his related observation that it is from "the *first* satisfying object" that a human being "learns to cognize" (1895, p. 331). In my opinion, the collective evidence regarding transitional relatedness points to the possibility, if not likelihood, that the primal cathexis of the "mothering One" is a special form of relatedness—analogous or identical to imprint learning—and does not follow the same maturational laws as later attachments. This attachment, unlike other forms of object relatedness, does not require the participation of later-developing ego functions to be mentally represented and is uniquely expressed in transitional object behavior.

Based on evidence to be presented regarding the essential connection between the existence of a maternal primary process presence and postinfancy transitional relatedness, I suggest that it is reasonable to assume that the onset of transitional relatedness, whether at one month or one year, is a sign of the establishment of a stable evocative image of the soothing mother. The infant's spontaneous groping for the preferred diaper, blanket, or piece of fuzz is an externalization of an established mode of tension relief that represents the infant's maternal percept.

"Associative connection" and "symbolic connection"

"Associative" connection denotes the child's ability to permit "spill-over" of the soothing experience with the mother before the capacity for symbolization has developed. "Symbolic" connection refers to the unconscious equation of the transitional object or a part of the object (e.g., its fur or softness) with the mother or a part of her (e.g., her hair or breast). The person is, when employing symbolism, "already clearly distinguishing between fantasy and fact, between inner objects and external objects, between primary creativity and perception" (Winnicott 1971, p. 6). These ego abilities—the ability to distinguish between inner and outer, etc.—move the child beyond the stage of mere associative connection. Because of these abilities, the child consciously knows that differences exist between the mother and the teddy bear. Unconsciously, the identity is asserted.

This relationship "facilitates engagement with novel, conflictual, even frightening circumstances"

The phrase, "this [the transitional] relationship facilitates engagement with novel, conflictual, even frightening circumstances" describes a well-known characteristic of the transitional mode. Some children can leave home happily only if they are allowed to bring along their treasured soother; many children have great difficulty sleeping without their special object; distress is a frequent stimulus for the use of the transitional object by both children and adults.

"Mediates or catalyzes psychological growth"

The phrase "mediates or catalyzes psychological growth" has been explicated by Coppolillo (1976): "I should like to claim for the transitional phenomenon a greater significance than has been accorded to it. I would maintain that the ability to experience in the transitional mode is essential for optimal ego development and important in man's striving to achieve resonance with his culture." Defining the transitional area of experience as "an ideal arena" for the mixing of internal and external realities, Coppolillo (1976) explains: "To have an object available in this way [to be experienced transitionally] is invaluable for the ego because it affords it a great deal of control. If the drive component becomes too imperative, the ego can cathect the realistic qualities of the object. If, conversely, the reality becomes too oppressive or boring, more of the inner world of wishes is permitted into awareness." Relationship to an object in the transitional mode is accompanied by a feeling of maximal security even in the face of novel, conflictual, frightening, or challenging circumstances. The emotional "refueling" (Mahler 1975, pp. 39–120) that accrues from the transitional relationship encourages renewed efforts at mastery.

The next chapter will contrast transitional relatedness and modes of experience with which it may be confused. The remainder of the definition—that is, of transitional relatedness as a lifelong developmental process—will be discussed in chapter 4.

Transitional Relatedness Contrasted with Other Forms of Emotional Relatedness

3

Let us now compare and contrast this unique ego function, the ability for transitional relatedness, with other modes of experience (i.e., pleasurable daydreaming, transference, being in love, play, ego-ideal gratification, and sublimation). The other states Coppolillo mentions—pure learning, interest, and fascination (Coppolillo 1976, p. 46)—arc simply too cognitive, too one-sidedly intellectual, to require differentiation from transitional relatedness as defined herein. Of these, "fascination" suggests or connotes the strongest cathexis of objects qua objects. However, it also connotes excitement and loss of ego autonomy, as when one is enchanted or in a spell. Finally, since there is an almost reflexive tendency in psychoanalysis to invoke narcissism and its transformations as an explanatory framework for transitional phenomena, I shall discuss this in the last section of this chapter.

Other modes of experience

Pleasurable daydreaming

Like transitional relatedness, the daydream may provide relief from difficulties, stress, even pain. And the daydream, like any other thing, may become the object of the transitional mode. However, the daydreaming mode itself is not the same as the transitional mode. For one, the relief of tension provided by daydreaming is unreliable. The initially pleasurable fantasy may wander into disruptive anxiety-laden ideas, whereas the transitional mode is, in health, a function of an ego that is "in excellent control and experiencing its finest hour" (Coppolillo 1976, p. 44). Throughout life the transitionally experiencing ego is the homeostatic, content ego.

Coppolillo (1976, p. 43) has stated that one difference between fantasy and the transitional phenomenon is that "in the process of fantasizing, there is no reliable representative of external reality . . .; how different this is from the soothing effects of the transitional object." Although this is usually correct, there is an important exception: Transitional relatedness, when it involves intangibles such as tunes, prayers, imaginary companions, etc., does not depend on an actual reliable representative of external reality. It may only seem to the person that the object is reliably external. Certainly the presence of a reliable representative of external reality is not characteristic of mature transitional relatedness, as I will show in the next chapter.

A second way in which transitional relatedness may be distinguished from the soothing daydream is that the latter removes one from action in the external world. As previously stated, transitional relatedness normally promotes engagement. The child, with the aid of his treasured soother, can leave home or endure the bombing of London; Cro-Magnon man, with the aid of his artwork deep in the recesses of limestone caves, can find solace and courage to face a hostile, dangerous world (Modell 1968); the composer with the aid of the music he plays or creates and the author with the aid of the essays he writes find themselves in closer contact with the culture they may neurotically fear. Daydreaming, with its closeness to egocentric primary process ideation (Schafer 1968, p. 89), is more characteristically asocial than transitional relatedness, which promotes interaction with the environment or, in a word, *relatedness*. Many daydreams express blatantly sexual or grandiose impulses—impulses that may serve to disrupt the transitional experience. Finally, the daydream leads to a suspension of reflective self-representations (Shafer 1968, p. 93): "It may be said of the daydream that it is satisfying or pleasurable in so far as the daydreamer temporarily or intermittently falls asleep in the course of it." Contrast this with, for example, the transitionally experiencing artist who is comfortingly aware of him or herself, the environment, and the area of merger—the work of art—between them.

Transference

Transference is an activity similar to transitional relatedness in that it seeks to bring about some degree of comfort. It is the path of least resistance for encountering new people or situations. The present is judged by the past, and the tension of a potentially new encounter is unconsciously obviated by the use of attitudes, perceptual modes, and ways of feeling that were hard-won during childhood but are now sometimes, but not always and certainly not predictably, comfortingly habitual. Coppolillo (1976, p. 44) has explained why transference—a mode of psychic activity in which wishes and impulses are represented—should not be confused with transitional relatedness: "In the case of transference, the ego is always in a helpless position and prey to at least signal anxiety. More fundamentally, I believe that in the case of transference ... the ego either is in constant danger or is actually overwhelmed by impulse life and therefore can be in a state of discomfort." The transference reaction, while at times reducing tension, does not characteristically provide solace, is not consciously sought, and, in effect, is a denial of the uniqueness, the freshness, and the creative possibilities of the present encounter. The fact that transference behavior is often unpredictably painful in its results is one reason that a person may decide to enter psychotherapy. To relate transferentially is to be a prisoner of one's illness, ignorance, laziness, or immaturity. In contrast, when the child cuddles the stuffed animal or the artist picks up his brush, these are activities consciously chosen with a firm expectation of comfort.

Being in love

Transitional relatedness and being in love may be mistaken for one another because they are identical during early childhood. The child finds solace through psychological union with things that stand for the relationship with the soothing mother. This relationship, it may be recalled, is virtually, if not actually, imprinted on the child during the first months of life. The psychological internalization of this relationship initiates a lifelong quest to bring about a *state of identity*, that is, to find objects that in one way or another are resonant with the soothing maternal primary process presence.

While the child favors certain objects by making them "come alive" with aspects of the self, his or her way of "loving" is clearly exploitative. Transitional objects offer solace or they cease to function as such. The special object—animate or inanimate—must remain unchallenging and unchanging. It is permitted no individuality except for that which its owner confers. When this mode of loving is carried into adult life it makes for many problems. Typical are the comments of this forty-year-old divorced woman about her transitionally fixated husband: "As long as I remained in the house, you know, 'pregnant and barefoot,' there was no problem. But as soon as I began to show involvement outside the house, that's where the difficulty began. It was threatening to him." Many men and women—but more often men—suffer great pain and anguish from the gradual or sudden loss of their human teddy bear. The complaint that I hear from some women about being exploited as "sex objects" is often mistaken. The immature men in their lives demand sex when what they really want, at a deeper, less conscious level, is regressive soothing. It would be much easier for these women if they could be treated as exciting sexual objects, full of mystery and surprise, rather than as objects of compulsive solace seeking.

Teddy-bear love in adult life can be decidedly pathological: A fifty-eight-year-old depressed mother of two—married for thirty-one years—stated that her husband "resented" her visits to me. Moreover, he didn't like it if she was talking on the telephone, watching television or reading a book, or, in short, doing anything that made her temporarily unavailable to him. This was true whether or not he had a specific need for her at that moment. He wanted her to be uninterruptedly accessible and aware of him. Regarding their first son, he had stated repeatedly over the years: "When John was born, I died." He meant by this that his wife now shared herself in an important way with another person. This was intolerable to him. He had tried very hard, all of his married life, to drive his wife and sons apart. About this she commented: "He doesn't want me to be shared with anybody or anything."

The above man was diagnosed to be suffering from the borderline syndrome (see also Arkema 1981). His unmodulated transitional object way of loving is similar to that of the small child.

These and other pathological distortions notwithstanding, there is an essential role for transitional relatedness in love at every stage in life. Being "in love" requires the transitional capacity for feeling joined but separate. Thus, there is the "coming alive" of inanimate objects as well as of nature and art that is so often part of the love experience (see Kernberg 1974).

Also to be considered is the fact that most adults need from time to time, and particularly when under stress, to have someone in whom they can find themselves and who, for that time, is uncritically accepting. Just as the child needs the solacing teddy bear to facilitate an awareness of certain inner states—to allow the child to orient him or herself to what is psychologically paramount at the moment—the adult requires another person to help relieve the lifelong strain of internal and external separateness.

An example of a young adult's need for a human transitional object in the context of a love relationship may be taken from *David Copperfield*. The youthful Copperfield said of his child-wife, Dora: "All this time I had gone on loving Dora harder than ever. Her idea was my refuge in disappointment and distress, and made some amends to me even for the loss of my friend. The more I pitied myself, or pitied others, the more I sought for consolation in the image of Dora. The greater the accumulation of deceit and trouble in the world, the brighter and purer shone the star of Dora high above the world."

In claiming that transitional relatedness *is* the small child's way of loving, and that it is an essential part of adult love, I am not overlooking the many ways in which mature love differs from simple transitional relatedness. Being in love implies the existence of sexual and aggressive excitement during at least some phases of the relationship—qualities not present in the emotionally well-balanced transitional state. Being in love may also result in an impairment of the lover's reflective self-representation, as when he or she has no concern for the self; *Romeo and Juliet* exemplifies the ecstasy of suicide that may accompany passionate love.

Other elements of being in love are commitment, caring, acceptance, respect, sharing, joy, and growth (Kaplan 1973). While the loved one may be used temporarily as a figurative teddy bear, he or she is not tossed away until needed again. Awareness of the reality of the other person as a separate, sentient human being is never completely suspended or forgotten. The soothing one is granted his or her turn to be demanding, egocentric, disappointing, weak, perverse, even hurtful without automatic penalty. Disillusionment is never total, and those who are truly in love sustain the capacity for mutually soothing union that transcends mere genital satisfaction.

An emphasis on the last-mentioned capacity—that of affording mutually soothing psychological union—is the quality that may lead to confusion of transitional relatedness with love. Indeed, there are occasions in any mature loving relationship on which transitional solace is center stage. A good example is David Copperfield's use of Dora as a transitional object. Confusion is dispelled when it is recognized that solace seeking is only part of a larger complex of attitudes, behaviors, and experiences that we call being in love.

Summarizing, the child's way of loving the teddy bear persists as a very important and essential component of mature adult love. A capacity for soothing psychological merger with things external is the foundation on which all healthy human relationships are built. In describing this mode of loving—a mode that is derivative of the early psychological union with the mother—it is to be emphasized that the "teddy bear" is merely one of the earliest, and symbolic of a great many objects, animate and inanimate, to which people may become attached throughout life. Developmentally, it is the mode of loving rather than the object that is crucial. In normal childhood teddy-bear love, the child imbues the treasured soother with the life he or she feels stirring inside of himself. The teddy bear's existence in this special "loving" relationship permits soothing projection of personal qualities that will eventually be claimed as part of the conscious self.

Severely personality-disordered individuals fail to develop this ability and remain emotionally isolated; schizophrenic persons are fixated at, or regress to, excessive attachment to concrete, tangible soothers; narcissistically disturbed patients often relate to the self-concept as though it were a teddy bear. Less pathological is the adult's rigid use of another person as a figurative teddy bear. He or she requires the loved one to be unremittingly soothing and accepting of projective needs and identifications. These borderline syndrome patients experience anxiety attacks and depression when their human teddy bear inevitably disappoints. Then, disillusionment is total—at least for a while—and the figurative teddy bear may be tossed away for a substitute soother.

Normal adult love also gives expression to certain aspects of the teddy-bear mode of loving. However, the healthy transitional mode vis-à-vis its reciprocal relationship to other ego functions leads to a greater awareness of and respect for the unique qualities of the solacing vehicle.

Play

At the Spring 1978 meeting of the American Psychoanalytic Association, Nathaniel London, M.D., had some interesting things to say about play:

> Dr. Horton's paper ["Transitional Relatedness as a Developmental Line"] reminds us not only of the importance of fantasy play for the organization of reality, for the development of mental organization and the relation of play to various forms of creativity, but also to the soothing and restorative aspects of play and fantasy. Yet, in Winnicott's classic article, a distinction between play and the transitional mode is blurred.

Certainly these complex behaviors overlap. Consider a
five-year-old girl—she happened to be a bed wetter—who
used her urine-smelling old blanket as a beautiful veil as she
played at being a bride. This fantasy play is quite different
from the times when this same little girl would clutch the
blanket with one hand and tug at her ear lobe with the other.
It would be only partly correct to conclude that the use of the
blanket as a *transitional object* underwent a *change of function* for its use in fantasy play. It would be more accurate to
observe that the use of the blanket in the bridal game marked
an intersection of this girl's line of development with respect
to fantasy play. . . . The distinction or overlap of play and transitional behaviors still needs to be clarified.

London correctly points out the change of function that occurs
when the blanket goes from being used as a transitional object to
being used as a toy. (See also my earlier discussion of the multiple
functions of objects.) And he is also right in stating that play and
transitional relatedness "intersect." But they certainly do not
overlap. In general, play is an aggressive, assertive, mastery-
seeking activity. Often physically vigorous and exciting, it is re-
hearsal for involvement with the external world and an avenue for
discharge of tension. In contrast, the transitional experience is
soothingly homeostatic; it is a psychological way station between
deep and dreamless sleep and all-out efforts at engagement with
the world. Relaxed play may shade over into the transitional experience (or vice versa), but when one begins the other ends.
Whereas use of the toy is an expression of the child's modulated
and socialized aggressive drive, and use of the fetishistic object is
an expression of defense against the libidinous drive, use of the
transitional object is an expression of the soothing maternal primary process presence—the foundation on which all later healthy
object relations are built (Jacobson 1964).

Ego-ideal activities

The satisfaction of the ego ideal may be confused clinically with
satisfaction in the transitional mode, since both satisfactions are
the product of goal-seeking activity. However, there are impor-

tant subjective differences between these superficially similar states. Transitional satisfaction is soothing, whereas ego-ideal gratification is exhilarating. The predominantly comforting quality that results from action in the transitional mode separates it subjectively from the "sitting on top of the world," "flying high," and "being on cloud nine" quality of ego-ideal attainment.

Metapsychologically, there are important differences between ego-ideal and transitional phenomena. The gratification obtained through the ego ideal results from dipping down, as Blos (1974) points out, into the amorphous and fluid state of primary narcissism. It must be recalled that, for Blos and other classical analysts, primary narcissism in the adult is the residual psychological condition of the infant characterized by primitive feelings—often disturbing to oneself and others—of omniscience and omnipotence.

In contrast, transitional activity does not draw gratification from experience of that residual of "primary narcissism" called the "grandiose self." Rather, it is never primarily egocentric in origin but always contains elements of a significant *other* that refines, modulates, and channels contaminating aspects of nonoceanic primary narcissism.

This is not meant to imply that there is necessary conflict between the "ego ideal" and the aim of the transitional mode. Some ego-ideal activities, especially artistic ones, may be, as it were, nurturant to the transitional mode. At other times the ego ideal may be little more than a contaminant of a complex activity that is oriented mainly toward the achievement of satisfaction in the transitional mode. Of course, a manifestly antisocial ego ideal may conflict with efforts at transitional relatedness due to instinctual disruptiveness.

Sublimation

Whereas sublimation is a *defense* against instinctual drives, transitional relatedness is an *expression*—often a fairly direct one—of a noninstinctual force, that is, the soothing maternal primary process presence. Sublimation is a diversionary activity; transitional relatedness is a vehicle for manifesting.

Social or cultural acceptability is not a defining feature of transitional relatedness. The child who insists on dragging his tattered blanket to the grocery story is neither sublimating nor showing much interest in what others may think. At a more advanced stage, the composer who steadfastly maintains that his music has value though the public refuses to listen is at least partly correct. The need to do it for its own sake—a characteristic of transitional relatedness—may be sufficient grounds for transitional activity.

Transitional relatedness, appearing as it does during the first few months of life, antedates even the most primitive defenses. The initial function of transitional relatedness is to permit mastery of separation from the mother. Later in life its central role is to facilitate self-object merger with objects other than the actual mother; it is always a combatant of the worst of all evils—aloneness, existential or otherwise.

The psychopathic woman described in the introduction was able to sublimate in a limited way, although she could not experience soothing self-object merger. She attempted to ward off the hell of loneliness by immersing herself in sado-masochistic instinctual activities and by defending herself in her work and play. On the other hand, transitional objects may be used by those who have little if any ability to sublimate. Examples were given at the end of the first chapter of patients who utilized predominantly "narcissistic" (Vaillant 1971) defenses but were able, nonetheless, to take objects into the intermediate area.

Why narcissism and its transformations do not explain transitional phenomena

This must be discussed, because narcissism is coming to replace the instincts as the ultimate psychological reality in psychoanalysis and, to some extent, in psychiatry. When I have presented my ideas on transitional relatedness to psychoanalytic-psychiatric forums, I have been either encouraged to relate them to narcissism or told categorically that narcissism explains these phenomena.

Kohut, the single most important driving force behind the narcissism movement, has suggested significant alterations in Freud's deceptively simple schema:

autoerotism————▸primary narcissism————▸object love

secondary narcissism◂— — — — —┘

Kohut finds that Freud's theory is inadequate to explain how the child reacts to disturbances of primary narcissism. (See especially Ornstein [1975] for a more complete summary of Kohut's thought; see also Horton 1978.) Rather than enlarging and refining the theory of object relations, Kohut has postulated not one but *two* additional developmental lines. These proposed separate developmental lines of narcissism may be schematized as follows:

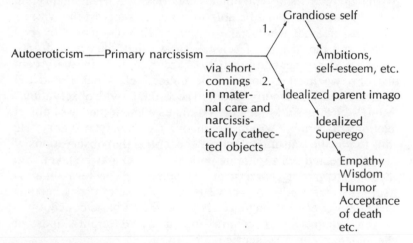

Each of these narcissistic transformations is thought to result from "transmuting internalization," a form of structure building that occurs when object-instinctual and narcissistic cathexes are withdrawn from objects.

Kohut also rejects the idea of a death instinct:

> Destructive rage, in particular, is always motivated by an injury to the self. The deepest level to which psychoanalysis can penetrate when it traces destructiveness . . . is not reached when it has been able to uncover a destructive biological

drive, is not reached when the analysand has become aware of the fact that he wants (or wanted) to kill. This awareness is but an intermediate station on the road to the psychological "bedrock": to the analysand's becoming aware of the presence of a serious narcissistic injury, an injury that threatened the cohesion of the self, especially a narcissistic injury inflicted by the self-object of childhood. [Pp. 116–17]

Thus, Kohut moves away from classical drive theory (Kohut 1977, p. xiii) and essentially abandons a psychoanalytic theory of object relations for the explanation of the phenomena he describes.

Not everybody is content with the abandonment of the classical psychoanalytic theory of object relations: "A rival theory, in order to be viable, must be able to compete successfully with its predecessor.... It would take a man of Freud's genius to rival Freud, and the history of science shows that such men do not appear in every generation; they scarcely appear in every century. So we must attempt to do collectively what Freud did singlehandedly, to modify theory in accordance with observation" (Modell 1968, p. 6). Modell then outlines a latent theory of object relations discernible within Freudian psychoanalytic theory. He adds to this the transitional object concept so that observations of "borderline and schizophrenic patients" (p. x) may be taken into account. Regarding narcissism, he opines: "The term 'narcissism' as a descriptive adjective is indispensable; it has become part of our everyday language. However, as a basic concept it is ...too complex and covers too many different kinds of phenomena to be fully serviceable" (p. 9).

Modell's criticism—that narcissism has been stretched to its conceptual breaking point—is well taken. An example of this overextension is Kohut's (1966) identification of wisdom, humor, empathy, creativity, and acceptance of death as ultimate transformations of narcissism. Does it make sense to try to explain complicated relationships to objects mainly by reference to a psychological state that is fundamentally inimical to the recognition of objects? The condition of primary narcissism, with its qualities

of grandiosity, omnipotence, and omniscience and its denial of
the I-thou distinction, recalls Freud's (1915) statement that
"hate . . . is older than love. It derives from the narcissistic ego's
primordial repudiation of the external world . . ." (p. 139). Suc-
cinctly put, too much implausible transforming has to go on to
make narcissism "fully serviceable."

The clinical and theoretical overextension of the narcissistic
theory of human relatedness is a result, in part, of the absence of
a limit-setting underlying philosophy. Let us take for examination
the idea that "acceptance of death" is a sign of maturity—an
ultimate transformation of narcissism (Kohut 1966). I have difficulty with two words in the phrase "acceptance of death,"
neither of which is a preposition. When we "accept death," just
exactly what are we doing? The classical psychoanalyst would
say that acceptance of death means the calm recognition that
when a person dies he or she is totally annihilated, that is, returned to a state of inorganic dissolution. It is this philosophical
framework—this logical positivism—that leads Eissler to regard
Beethoven's death mask as proof of the ultimate extinction of a
great soul and Lidz (1973) to comment:

> Awareness that life in itself is without meaning is no new
> existential insight, as a reading of Ecclesiastes shows; and wis-
> dom, to many non-religious oriented existentialists, has meant
> accepting the inherent meaninglessness of the universe and
> finding a way to make the one-time venture of living person-
> ally worthwhile. To many, this search has meant learning how
> to cultivate deep and meaningful relationships, and to live in
> the light of some ideal that transcends the self—perhaps by
> seeking to make life more satisfactory or rewarding for
> others—while the world continues through its meaningless
> orbit, and even as nations and cultures rise and fall. [P. 129]

Frankly, I do not understand how anyone can say, with any
degree of conviction, that life is "meaningless" and that the utter
annihilation of every intangible that a human cherishes is a reality
that is "accepted" by the truly "mature" person. Allowing that
Freud, Eissler, Kohut, and Lidz may be correct, I find the

axiomatic nature of their statements puzzling. Paradoxically, their knowledge of these matters—if valid—would be virtually miraculous.

The narcissistic explanation of all human relationships, including the relationship with death, is perfectly suited to the nineteenth-century logical positivism of Auguste Comte and to Freud's reaffirmation of it in the opening paragraph of his "Project for a Scientific Psychology." It is a dense, thoroughgoing, untransitional way of grounding human values. Clinically, it is killing to the human spirit. It is a nihilism whose propagation in a healing context should require extraordinary justification.

Transitional Relatedness as a Lifelong Developmental Process

4

In the preceding chapter I stated that for most people transitional relatedness is a developmental line, that is, a growth process and series of changes, often lifelong, which is influenced by experience and arises out of the interaction of maturational and environmental elements. At first glance the essence of this developmental process is the capacity for soothing illusion formation. However, at a deeper level it is the existence of a nonillusory soothing maternal primary process presence that is quintessential.

In discussing an abbreviated version of this chapter, Kavka (1978) opined that Winnicott "may have regarded transitional phenomena as life-long processes but did not postulate a developmental line of *illusion* . . . [and] . . . provided only the vaguest outlines of developmental possibilities which Dr. Horton now boldly extends." Kavka's interpretation certainly has support. In the American Psychoanalytic Association's *Glossary of Psychoanalytic Terms and Concepts,* the transitional object is defined as "the infant's first possession." While acknowledging that the transitional object may be exceptionally present throughout life, it is described in the *Glossary* as a potential "point of departure for abnormal developments." Tolpin's (1971) point of view is even more restrictive. She states that the soothing function of the blanket undergoes a process of "transmuting internalization" leading to a "genuine 'passing' of the transitional

An abbreviated version of this chapter was presented at the Spring meeting of the American Psychoanalytic Association in Atlanta, Georgia, 1978.

object" and confines transitional relatedness, by definitional fiat, to the pre-oedipal period. Volkan (1972) takes a similarly narrow stance when he claims that the transitional object is a transitory manifestation at the pre-oedipal level (p. 220). Perhaps this emphasis took its origin from Anna Freud's (1963) reductionistic interpretation of Winnicott's concept. She defined the transitional object as merely the "infant's first plaything" (p. 258) and referred to the disturbed children who "cling" to these objects or modes of relatedness.

On the other hand, we have the following remarks by Winnicott to consider: "I am therefore studying the substance of *illusion*, that which is allowed to the infant, and which in adult life is inherent in art and religion, and yet becomes the hallmark of madness when an adult puts too powerful a claim on the credulity of others, forcing them to acknowledge a sharing of illusion that is not their own. We can share a respect for *illusory experience*, and if we wish we may collect together and form a group on the basis of the similarity of our illusory experiences. This is a natural root of grouping among human beings" (p. 3).

Statements such as the above have led me to conclude that Winnicott was contemplating not only the illusory but also the developmental possibilities that will emerge in this chapter. Stone (1966) too seems to be on the same track that I am when he interprets Winnicott's concept of the transitional object to refer to the "subsequent enduring and pervasive role of illusion in human mental life" (p. 52). However, I agree with Kavka that the developmental possibilities to which Winnicott refers were only explored in a preliminary and therefore necessarily somewhat vague manner.

Since the advent of ego psychology, there has been a strong tendency to emphasize the differences between the adult and the child: the hierarchization of defenses that culminates in sublimation, altruism, and humor (Vaillant 1972); the transformation of narcissism that leads to wisdom (Kohut 1966); the cognitive unfolding that results in the capacity for abstraction (Piaget 1969); the transmuting internalization that eliminates the need for transitional relatedness (Tolpin 1971); etc.

Our professional fascination with ego development may be
making it difficult to see the many ways in which childish elements and modes persist even in healthy adult life. Actually,
there is considerable psychoanalytic precedent for the acknowl-
edgment of the perpetuation of childhood functioning in adulthood. The "complemental series" (Freud 1893) and "regression
in the service of the ego" (Kris 1952) underpin Schafer's (1968)
statement that "adults continuously long to be children once
again at play, remaking the world to suit their wishes and quiet
their fears" (p. 87). Schafer also reminds us of Freud's study of
jokes and Kris's elaboration to the effect that "the childhood
mode of function itself is pleasurable, apart from the content it
deals with..."

The psychoanalysts appear to be echoing, in part, observations
made in the last century by people such as Wordsworth, who
noted pithily that "the child is father of the man," and Dickens,
who commented:

> I think the memory of most of us can go further back into such
> times [early childhood] than many of us suppose, just as I be-
> lieve the power of observation in numbers of very young chil-
> dren to be quite wonderful for its closeness and accuracy. In-
> deed, I think that most grown men who are remarkable in this
> respect, may with greater propriety be said not to have lost
> the faculty, than to have acquired it; the rather as I generally
> observe such men to retain a certain freshness, and gentle-
> ness, and capacity of being pleased, which are also an inher-
> itance they have preserved from their childhood. [*David
> Copperfield*]

The statement by Dickens may also serve as an introduction to
an extended literary example of lifelong transitional relatedness.
However, before proceeding with an analysis of the transitional
mode in *David Copperfield* there is one more quotation regarding
the persistence of childlike modes and contents which I would
like to share. The great filmmaker Ingmar Bergman, who himself
shows a curious mixture of youthful charm, vulnerability, and
ferocious intensity, said: "Many artists' faces are like the faces of
grown-up, secretive children. Look at a face like Picasso's! It's a

child's face. Or Churchill or the Swedberg [Swedish chemist and Nobel prizewinner]—another kid who's never grown up. Or Stravinsky, or Orson Welles, or Hindemith. One might even add a man like Mozart—but admittedly we don't know exactly what Mozart looked like—but from his pictures we can be sure it was so. Even Beethoven's face. One could call it the face of a wrathful infant" (1973, p. 84).

There are conflicting points of view regarding the appropriateness of using literary and other non-case-study material to illustrate and substantiate psychological constructs. A conservative position is that of Greenacre (1957), who claims that it is an "illusion" (p. 48) to think that biographers and autobiographers can present the subject without "gross distortions" and "startling omissions." She allows, though, that "the true artist may be more faithful with deeper inner integrity in his relation to his collective audience than he is with his personal connections" (p. 50). Husserl (1962), too, thought that the artist might excel in the portrayal of the "systematic continuity of motive forces"—a position with which I am in agreement.

The autobiography of Charles Dickens commends itself to our attention, not only because of its originality, abundance of detailed features, and description of motive forces, but also because David Copperfield's life—the life of a genius—is, as it were, a veritable exercise in transitional relatedness.

As the book opens, we learn that David's father died before his birth. His loving mother, in need of companionship and financial support, eventually marries a man who proves to be exceptionally sadistic and controlling. At age eight David is forced by his stepfather, Murdstone, into virtual isolation from his well-intentioned but overwhelmed mother. In his sadness he seeks soothing:

> The natural result of this treatment, continued I suppose for some six months or more, was to make me sullen, dull and dogged. I was not made the less so by my sense of being daily more and more shut out and alienated from my mother. I believe I should have been almost stupefied but for one circumstance. . . . My father had left a small collection of books in a little room upstairs, to which I had access (for it adjoined my

own), and which nobody else in our house ever troubled.
From that blessed little room, Roderick Random, Peregrine
Pickle, Humphrey Clinker, Tom Jones, the Vicar of
Wakefield, Don Quixote, Gil Blas, and Robinson Crusoe,
came out, a glorious host, to keep me company. They kept
alive my fancy, and my hope of something beyond that place
and time—they, and the Arabian Nights, and the Tales of the
Genii—and did me no harm; for whatever harm was in some
of them was not there for me—I knew nothing of it. It is astonishing to me now how I found time, in the midst of my
porings and blunderings over heavier themes, to read those
books as I did. It is curious to me how I could ever have
consoled myself under my small troubles (which were great
troubles to me), by impersonating my favourite characters in
them—as I did—and by putting Mr. & Miss Murdstone into all
the bad ones—which I did too. I have been Tom Jones (a
child's Tom Jones, a harmless creature) for a week together. I
have sustained my own idea of Roderick Random for a month
at a stretch, I verily believe. I had a greedy relish for a few
volumes of Voyages and Travels—I forget what, now—that
were on those shelves; and for days and days I can remember
to have gone about my region of our house, armed with the
centrepiece out of an old set of boot-trees—the perfect re-
alization of Captain Somebody, of the Royal British Navy, in
danger of being beset by savages, and resolved to sell his life
at a great price. The Captain never lost dignity, from having
his ears boxed with the Latin Grammar. I did; but the Captain
was a captain and a hero, in despite of all the grammars of all
the languages in the world, dead or alive. This was my only
and my constant comfort. [Pp. 58–59]

Many elements of transitional relatedness are perspicuous in
the above quotation. David is alienated from his mother and very
sad. He requires a vehicle for solace. Some soothing objects—
books that belonged to his father—are readily available. These
books are also connected with his mother. She gave them to him.
Indeed, all that David knew of his father came to him through his
mother. These vehicles for solace—these transitional objects—
became his "only and constant comfort." And, like any consoling
object, they facilitated adaptation. Through them he was able to

modulate his hatred and aggressive strivings toward the odious sadists his mother depended on. Partly he identified with the various humane and heroic characters in the books. He also achieved relief through imagining future vindications and gratifications. All in all, Copperfield's relationship with the books gave him greater *autonomy*—as Coppolillo might emphasize—from internal drive states and abrasively disheartening external circumstances.

Why don't I simply call the above an example of pleasurable fantasy, or play, or fascination, or intense interest, or adaptive identification, or something else? The answer takes us back to the definitional chapter. It is the special *cohesion* of factors that makes it transitional relatedness—separation from the mother, the use of objects that in some way stand for or are connected with her, the occurrence of reliable soothing, the development of greater freedom from oppressive circumstances, internal and/or external, and the facilitation of an adaptive solution to an otherwise overwhelming conflict.

Fantasy, identification, play, fascination, and other activities are indeed present and coordinate with David's transitional mode. They are psychological activities appropriate to a bright latency-aged youngster.

The assertion that the books represent or unconsciously symbolize David's mother is reinforced by the events that follow. After his mother's death David is cared for by his beloved Peggotty, a kindly maternal surrogate of whom his mother was quite fond. Unfortunately, David is soon deprived of her company also by the same Murdstones who had committed soul murder on his mother. Being seldom allowed to visit with Peggotty, David notes: "All this time I was so conscious of the waste of any promise I had given, and of my being utterly neglected, that I should have been perfectly miserable, I have no doubt, but for the old books. They were my only comfort, and I was as true to them as they were to me, and read them over and over I don't know how many times more" (p. 159).

At ten years of age David summoned up another crucial and this time blatantly maternal transitional object:

Sleep came upon me as it came on many other outcasts, against whom house-doors were locked and house-dogs barked that night—and I dreamed of lying on my old school bed, talking to the boys in my room; and found myself sitting upright, with Steerforth's name upon my lips, looking wildly at the stars that were glistening and glimmering above me. When I remembered where I was at that untimely hour, a feeling stole upon me that made me get up, afraid of I don't know what, and walk about. But the fainter glimmering of the stars, and the pale light in the sky where the day was coming, reassured me; and my eyes being very heavy, I lay down again and slept—though with a knowledge in my sleep that it was cold—until the warm beams of the sun, and the ringing of the getting-up bell at Salem House, awoke me.... What a different Sunday morning from the old Sunday morning at Yarmouth! In due time I heard the churchbells ringing, as I plodded on;... I felt quite wicked in my dirt and dust, and with my tangled hair. *But for the quiet picture I had conjured up of my mother in her youth and beauty weeping by the fire, and my aunt relenting to her, I hardly think I should have had courage to go on until next day. But it always went before me, and I followed.* [Pp. 192–93, italics added]

This gentle mitigation—the reliably saving image of "mother in her youth and beauty"—is reiterated:

This adventure frightened me so, that, afterwards, when I saw any of these people coming, I turned back until I could find a hiding-place, where I remained until they had gone out of sight; which happened so often that I was very seriously delayed. *But under this difficulty, as under all the other difficulties of my journey, I seemed to be sustained and led on by my fanciful picture of my mother in her youth, before I came into the world. It always kept me company. It was there, among the hops, when I lay down to sleep; it was with me on my waking in the morning; it went before me all day.* I have associated it, ever since, with the sunny street of Canterbury, dozing, as it were, in the hot light, and with the sight of its old houses and gateways, and the stately, grey cathedral, with the rooks sailing around the towers. When I came, at last, upon

the bare, wide downs near Dover, it relieved the solitary aspect of the scene with hope; and not until I reached that first
great aim of my journey, and actually set foot in the town
itself, on the sixth day of my flight, did it desert me. [P. 198,
italics added]

In the above quotation we find an unambiguous description of a
soothing maternal primary process presence—"[his] fanciful
picture of mother in her youth" that "always kept [him] company" and "relieved the solitary aspect[s] . . . with hope." Please
note that this presence is almost literally David's pathway into the
future and is given up when he reaches his destination and can
rest.

After I had said my prayers, and the candle had burnt out, I
remember how I still sat looking at the moonlight on the
water, as if I could hope to read my fortune in it, as in a bright
book; *or to see my mother with her child, coming from
Heaven, along that shining path, to look upon me as she had
looked when I last saw her sweet face.* I remember how the
solemn feeling with which at length I turned my eyes away,
yielded to the sensation of gratitude and rest which the sight
of the white-curtained bed—and how much more the lying
softly down upon it, nestling in the snow-white sheets!—
inspired. I remember how I thought of all the solitary places
under the night sky where I had slept, and how I prayed that I
never might be houseless any more, and might forget the
houseless.* I remember how I seemed to float, then, down the
melancholy glory of that track upon the sea, away into the
world of dreams. [Pp. 210–11, italics added]

---

* Freud (1900) relates a similar passage from Keller suggesting that the dream
itself may sometimes represent an *attempt* at transitional relatedness: "If you are
wandering about in a foreign land far from your home and from all that you hold
dear, if you have seen and heard many things, have known sorrow and care, and
are wretched and forlorn, then without fail you will dream one night that you are
coming near to your home; you will see it gleaming and shining in the fairest
colours, and the sweetest, dearest and most beloved forms will move towards
you . . ." (p. 246). See also the examples in the introduction of vehicles for solace
that appeared in dreams of my patients.

Not only does the shining, sentient image of his mother fortify him against the perils and sufferings of his lonely journey but, like any good transitional object, it helps him to fall asleep.

There is something else of import in this quotation. In the last chapter I stated that "to the extent that the maternal primary process presence is connected with the latent oceanic experience it is soothing." Here is an explicit connection: After he says his prayers, David Copperfield experiences his mother's presence—"coming from Heaven, along that shining path"— and, finally, "float[s]...down the melancholy glory of that track upon the sea, away into the world of dreams."

What were the circumstances that stimulated such elaborate and strongly invested transitional relatedness? David himself described them: "The remembrance of that life is fraught with so much pain to me, with so much mental suffering and want of hope, that I have never had the courage even to examine how long I was doomed to lead it. Whether it lasted for a year, or more or less, I do not know. I only know that it was, and ceased to be; and that I have written, and there I leave it" (p. 228). We see in this quote the anguish that so often precedes genuine efforts at transitional relatedness and that alerts us to the fact that the activity in question is not mere play, fantasy, daydreaming, or any other more simple condition, or any collection of them.

Let us move ahead to David's adolescence, where, as we might expect, his transitional activities have a new focus. He is more mature and has become interested in young women. He finds a series of "blue angels" (p. 285): "I adore Miss Shepherd...I cannot look upon my book, for I must look upon Miss Shepherd. When the choristers chant, I hear Miss Shepherd. In the service, I mentally insert Miss Shepherd's name; I put her in among the Royal Family. At home, in my own room, I am sometimes moved to cry out, 'Oh, Miss Shepherd!' in a transport of love" (p. 280).

After a while, David has relegated Miss Shepherd—the former one "pervading theme and vision of [his] life" (p. 281)—to limbo and has found a replacement in Miss Larkins, about whom he says: "Everything that belongs to her, or is connected with her, is precious to me" (p. 284). Other blue angels follow.

Why not call these relationships simple infatuations or the lustings of a naive young boy, or even "love"? Part of the answer lies in the quotations themselves, and the rest in surrounding issues as Dickens develops them. It is fairly apparent, I believe, that David does not lust after these women in the way that an adolescent boy might after a movie queen—these are "blue angels," not sexy starlets. Moreover, the visionary aspects have psychological importance beyond mere fantasy gratification or substitute masturbation. Miss Shepherd was, for a while, a "pervading theme and vision"—a persisting vivid conception, an object of imaginative contemplation that involved looking at the world from one particular perspective and not others. The perspective that David had was that these blue angels offered him solace—relief from the awful loneliness he had felt ever since his mother's death. Instinctual drives, as such, were not very apparent or significant in David's relatedness to these adored women.

True, he said he "loved" them. But, as I discussed in the last chapter, transitional relatedness *is* the young person's way of loving. Only later are other aims—among them those that are instinct-laden—added and can one truly be said to be capable of "loving." David knew so little of Miss Shepherd and Miss Larkins that love in the sense of a gestalt of attitudes and commitments to sharing, caring, accepting, growing with, and experiencing mutual joy were impossible. Consequently, he was easily disillusioned and soon learned that one must choose one's *human* transitional objects with greater care.

Perhaps David did not learn that lesson soon enough. He eventually married one of the blue angels, his ill-fated Dora. Childlike, emotionally weak and unstable, Dora nevertheless seemed to offer David the possibility of maternal soothing. In her timidity, sensitivity, tenderness, and exceptional vulnerability to life's stress she was after all very much like David's mother.

Dora was clearly used as a transitional object: "Her idea was my refuge in disappointment and distress, and made some amends to me even for the loss of my friend. The more I pitied myself, or pitied others, the more I sought for consolation in the image of Dora. The greater the accumulation of deceit and trouble

in the world, the brighter and the purer shone the star of Dora
high above the world'' (pp. 497–98).

Copperfield had multiple, concurrent transitional relationships.
Even while he remained attached to Dora, he related transitionally
to the woman who was to become his ultimate object, Agnes.

> I see her, with her modest, orderly, placid manner, and I
> hear her beautiful, calm voice, as I write these words. The
> influence for all good, which she came to exercise over me at
> a later time, begins already to descend upon my breast. I love
> little Em'ly, and I don't love Agnes—no, not at all in that
> way—but I feel there are goodness, peace, and truth wherever
> Agnes is; and that the soft light of the coloured window in the
> church, seen long ago, falls on her always, and on me when I
> am near her, and on everything around. [P. 244]

Returning to Canterbury as a man, Copperfield reflects on the
special transitional influence of Agnes and shows the ''coming
alive'' of inanimate objects that are associated with the serene
''silent presence'' (p. 827):

> Strange to say, that quiet influence which was inseparable in
> my mind from Agnes, seemed to pervade even the city where
> she dwelt. The venerable cathedral towers, and the old
> jackdaws and rooks whose airy voices made them more re-
> tired than perfect silence would have done; the battered gate-
> ways, once stuck full of statues, long thrown down and crum-
> bled away, like the reverential pilgrims who had gazed upon
> them; the still nooks, where the ivied growth of centuries
> crept over gabled ends and ruined walls; the ancient houses,
> the pastoral landscape of field, orchard and garden; *every-*
> *where—on everything—I felt the same serener air, the same*
> *calm, thoughtful, softening spirit.* [P. 593, italics added]

As a mature man, Copperfield could not have been more lucidly
expressive of Agnes's transitional meaning for him than he was in
the following lines:

> And now, indeed, I began to think that, in my old associa-
> tion of her with the stained-glass window in the church, a pro-
> phetic foreshadowing of what she would be to me, in the

calamity that was to happen in the fulness of time, had found a way into my mind. In all that sorrow, from the moment, never to be forgotten, when she stood before me with her upraised hand, *she was like a sacred presence in my lonely house.* When the Angel of Death alighted there, my child-wife fell asleep—they told me so when I could bear to hear it—on her bosom, with a smile. From my swoon, I first awoke to a consciousness of her compassionate tears, her words of hope and peace, *her gentle face bending down as from a purer region nearer Heaven, over my undisciplined heart, and softening its pain.* [P. 811, italics added]

The transitional formula repeats itself in the above quotation—loneliness, the search for a reliable soother, the felt *presence* of a maternal object, and a way into the future. The reader may not need reminding that David's mother too had once come to him "along that shining path"—from "Heaven" (pp. 210–11)—to console him and to "soften" his pain.

Agnes, unlike the other blue angels, remained psychologically vital for David: "I walked through the streets . . . and there meditated on Miss Shepherd and the eldest Miss Larkins, and all the idle loves and likings and dislikings of that time. Nothing seemed to have survived that time but Agnes, and she, ever a star above me, was brighter and higher" (p. 885). Miss Shepherd and Miss Larkins were not forgotten or their memory repressed, they were simply "relegated to limbo" (Winnicott 1953); David became disillusioned with them and moved on to a transitional object, Agnes, who offered greater play to his extraordinary sensitivities and need for consolation. His phrase, "idle loves," is a good one for discarded transitional objects.

As a middle-aged man, Copperfield continued to have his illusions about Agnes, who "with her own sweet tranquility . . . calmed [his] agitation" (p. 883): "You will always be my solace and resource, as you have always been. . . . I knew . . . that there was something inexplicably gentle and softened surrounding you . . ." (p. 888). And Copperfield's last words were a testimony to the uniquely vital role of the forward- (and upward-) looking transitional object:

And, now as I close my task, subduing my desire to linger
yet, these faces fade away. But one face, shining on me like a
Heavenly light by which I see all other objects, is above them,
and beyond them all. And that remains.

I turn my head, and see it, in its beautiful serenity, beside
me. My lamp burns low, and I have written far into the night;
but the dear *presence,* without which I were nothing, bears me
company.

O Agnes, O my soul! so may thy face be by me when I close
my life indeed; so may I, when realities are melting from me
like the shadows which I now dismiss, still find thee near me
pointing upward! [P. 923, italics added]

As stated earlier, Copperfield showed *multiple* transitional object relationships. His use of books and a series of blue angels
have been discussed. By and large the books were short-lived
transitional objects compared to his relationship with Agnes.
Even then the old books had some residual evocative transitional
capacity as exemplified by David's fond reference in middle age
to the "books that Agnes and [he] had read together" (p. 882).

Copperfield also related transitionally to at least two places of
residence, Mr. Peggotty's houseboat and his own first apartment
in London. The soothing that the houseboat—a perfect symbol of
the nurturant, oceanic mother—conferred had a more regressive
character than Agnes, who was "ever leading [him] to something
better; ever directing [him] to higher things!" (p. 887). (Please
recall Modell's description of the transitional object as having a
regressive as well as a progressive side.) Regarding the houseboat, Copperfield said: "After tea, when the door was shut and all
made snug (the nights being cold and misty now), it seemed to me
the most delicious retreat that the imagination of man could conceive. To hear the wind getting up out at sea, to know that the fog
was creeping over the desolate flat outside, and to look at the fire
and think that there was no house near but this one ..." (p. 34). In
late adolescence, Copperfield found an equivalent of his childhood residence: "It was a wonderfully fine thing to have that lofty
castle to myself, and to feel, when I shut my door, like Robinson
Crusoe, when he had got into his fortification, and pulled his

ladder up after him" (p. 374). In this quotation Copperfield links *two* transitional objects, one of his treasured books from latency and his soothing abode of adolescence.

Copperfield's memories of being safely ensconced in a maternal surround at different times in his life—his beloved Peggotty's houseboat and his "lofty castle" that reminded him of a "fortification"—bring to mind a report given by a sailor in our study on normal and personality-disordered transitional related-ness (Horton et al. 1974). Asked if he had had any special attachments in childhood, he said that he had many stuffed animals, liked to construct *forts* with them, crawl inside with his favorite animal, a bear, and pretend that he was safe from the Indians.

Correlatively, Heiman (1976) quotes Van Gogh as follows: "I have just said to Gauguin about this picture that when he and I were talking about the fishermen of Iceland and of the mournful isolation, exposed to all dangers, alone on the sad sea . . . the idea came to me to paint a picture in such a way that sailors, who are at once children and martyrs, seeing it in the cabin of their Icelandic fishing boat, would feel the old sense of being rocked come over them and remember their own lullabies." And we might also recall the words of the poet, W. B. Yeats:

> I will arise and go now, and go to Innisfree,
> And a small cabin build there, . . .
> And I shall have some peace there . . .

It is perhaps worth mentioning that Dickens described apparent *inanimate* transitional object usage by several other characters in *David Copperfield:* Mr. Micawber with his petition (p. 178), Mr. Dick with his "great kite" (p. 228), Dr. Strong with his "famous dictionary" (p. 266), and Mr. Barkis with his box are among the instances. The character development of Micawber and others is not, of course, as complete as it is with the main character, who speaks in the first person. Yet the nature of their relationships with their special objects is, if not conclusive of transitional re-latedness, at least highly suggestive:

> This veneration Mr. Dick extended to the Doctor, whom he thought the most subtle and accomplished philosopher of any

age. It was long before Mr. Dick ever spoke to him otherwise
than bareheaded; and even when he and the Doctor had struck
up quite a friendship, and would walk together by the hour, on
that side of the courtyard which was known among us as the
Doctor's walk, Mr. Dick would pull off his hat at intervals to
show his respect for wisdom and knowledge. How it ever
came about that the Doctor began to read scraps of the famous Dictionary, in these walks, I never knew; perhaps he
felt it all the same, at first, as reading to himself. However, it
passed into a custom too; and Mr. Dick, listening with a face
shining with pride and pleasure, in his heart of hearts, believed the Dictionary to be the most delightful book in the
world. [P. 266]

In this example, it is likely that the "famous dictionary" was a
shared transitional object between Mr. Dick and Doctor Strong,
two men very much in need of solace.

Mr. Barkis's box was a more private matter:

I may claim the merit of having originated the suggestion
that the will should be looked for in the box. After some
search, it was found in the box, at the bottom of a horse's
nose-bag; wherein (besides hay) there was discovered an old
gold watch, with chain and seals, which Mr. Barkis had worn
on his wedding-day, and which had never been seen before or
since; a silver tobacco-stopper, in the form of a leg; an imita-
tion lemon, full of minute cups and saucers, which I have
some idea Mr. Barkis must have purchased to present to me
when I was a child, and afterwards found himself unable to
part with; eighty-seven guineas and a half... an old horse-
shoe, a bad shilling, a piece of camphor, and an oyster shell.
From the circumstance of the latter article having been much
polished, and displaying prismatic colours on the inside, I
conclude that Mr. Barkis had some general ideas about pearls,
which never resolved themselves into anything definite.

For years and years Mr. Barkis had carried this box, on all
his journeys, every day. That it might the better escape
notice, he had invented a fiction that it belonged to "Mr.
Blackboy," and was "to be left with Barkis till called for"—a
fable he had elaborately written on the lid in characters now
scarcely legible. [P. 469]

The motive forces for Mr. Barkis's daily relationship with his
special box may be further revealed in his last words, words that
described his attitude about death: "Barkis is willin'!" and in
Dickens's comment, "And it being low water, he [Barkis] went
out with the tide" (p. 468). Mr. Barkis lived close to the ocean
and carried his vehicle for meaning and solace with him every day
of his adult life.

The developmental stages

Having presented an example that shows something of the full
range of healthy, even creative, transitional possibilities from latency to the middle years, I would like to turn now to an examination of the issues specific to each developmental phase.

Birth to age two

The blanket, diaper, soft toy, and piece of fuzz are among the
most frequently chosen first, manifest transitional objects. This
statement must be qualified with the word "manifest," because
we cannot, of course, rule out the possibility that there are purely
psychological transitional phenomena that precede the selection
of these soft objects. A hypothetical example of an infantile psychological transitional object might be in the relationship of the
infant to some internalized activity of the mother or to her imagined presence. I am led to postulate this partly on the basis of
having observed several children who, in addition to utilizing
palpable soothers, described, as soon as they were verbal
enough, the existence of soothing imaginary companions. These
children were in the latter part of the second year of life when
they were first able to make these transitional activities known.
We can only speculate as to how early these imaginary companions or their predecessors actually made their appearance.

In infancy the imagined presence "is the representation of the
good-enough mother in the manner of the relatively unmodified
primary process" (Schafer 1968, p. 123). The selection of the
blanket or diaper is a result of the crude differentiation of the

mother-infant relationship out of the fragmentary, fluid, and amorphous primary process experience. Familiarity, availability, physical texture, and smell of the soother are among factors that explain the infant's choice of soother (Busch et al. 1973).

Is the soother selected mainly for taste, texture, smell, warmth, or some combination thereof? Is it sucked, stroked, or cuddled? Is it held against cheek or lips or at a distance? Is it a blanket, diaper, piece of fuzz, or stuffed animal? Is it brightly colored or dull, heavy or light, big or small? Is it used in combination with other objects or activities? And why these differences? What Escalona (1963) has said more generally applies in understanding these early, extramaternal relationships: "Two categories of variables, environmental and organismic, converge and *reciprocally* interact in shaping the moment-by-moment and year-by-year experience of the growing child" (p. 242, italics added). More specifically, she points out that babies in the age range of seven months already "select those patterns of bodily self-stimulation which generate sensations in the same modalities that have characterized intense contacts with the mother in the past, when it was she who provided the stimulation." These conditioned modes of self-stimulation lead naturally to the choice of a particular soother or soothers.

The mother's role

The mother normally protects the psychological state of the infant, stimulating and encouraging growth along some lines while discouraging it along others. Commenting on this, Loewald (1962) has said: "[A] presumed omnipotent sufficiency appears to be maintained, for a time, by the close 'symbiotic' relationship with the mother" (p. 495). If the mother allows the development of an intensely stimulating and gratifying symbiosis, we may suppose that this is the basis of what is at first a conscious and later an unconscious sense of fusion with the *nurturant* breast-mother (to be contrasted with the negative, depriving, punitive, and hated mother).

It is the abiding sense of this nurturant breast-mother that may, after weaning, become conscious as a soothing primary process presence. Schafer (1968, p. 77) states that this "felt presence" serves the "interest of a maintained libidinal tie to the [mother]." The "good" other presence is experienced "even while the actual mother is 'known' to be involved in other matters."

Constitutional differences

Constitutional differences in activity level and perceptual sensitivity may be expected to play a role. One child at six months of age may rely mainly on orality in making contact with his chosen object whereas another child may blend touch, kinesthesis, and proprioception. Still another child may emphasize distance receptors in his construction of the maternal percept: "... in the great majority of cases the breast-fed baby stares at the face of the mother unswervingly throughout the act of nursing... until he falls asleep at the breast" (Spitz 1965, p. 51). In whatever way the first image of the mother is constructed (or whether it is constructed at all), we can be reasonably certain that it will consist of a collage of sensory experiences derived from preferred and conditioned modalities of sensation and that it, in turn, will inform the infant's choice of the transitional object and the manner in which it is used.

The psychological state of the infant

Let us look more closely at this nebulous psychological wilderness from which transitional activities first emerge. "Primary narcissism"—the "objectless stage" (Spitz 1965, p. 35) or "undifferentiated phase" (Hartmann 1939)—is the condition of "the infant [who] is as yet unaware of anything but his own experience of tension and relief, of frustration and gratification" (Jacobson 1964, p. 15). According to Kohut (1966), the phrase "primary narcissism... comprehends the assertion that the baby originally experiences the mother and her ministrations not as a you and its actions but within a view of the world in which the I-you differ-

entiation has not yet been established" (p. 245). The self at this
stage is presumed to be a constellation of "libidinal and aggressive forces in [an] undifferentiated 'psychosomatic' matrix [or, in
other words] the primal psycho-physiological self'" (Jacobson
1964, p. 6).

The existence of transitional relatedness at one or two months
of age must make us take pause regarding the validity of the
above statements. As soon as the mother—or, to be more precise,
some aspect of the mother—is psychologically internalized and
this internalization can activate transitional activities, the I-you
differentiation is manifestly established. The earliest psychological condition of the normal infant may, therefore, be much more
object-related than has been supposed.

Actually, there is much about the infant's psychological condition that is mysterious. The majority of an infant's life is passed in
a dozing, sleeping, passive state, and it is hypothesized that this is
experientially very much like the adult's sleep state. On the other
hand, infants, unlike adults, spend most of their sleep time in the
REM stage. If infants are dreaming, what are they dreaming
about and why do they spend so much time doing it?

Perhaps the blissful condition of the contentedly nursing infant,
which finds resonance in our own yearnings for a return to something like the Garden of Eden, is a reflection of the oceanic component of primary narcissism.

Individual differences in primary narcissism

Most psychoanalysts seem to have assumed that the primitive
unconscious—the repository of primary narcissism—is "relatively the same for everybody" (Fenichel 1945, p. 466). This conclusion, if not a revelation, was arrived at mainly by studying the
unconscious contents, styles, and conflicts that emerged during
the course of psychoanalytic treatment of adults. However, there
are two special contrasting groups of people who either do not
feel the need for psychoanalysis or who are unanalyzable, and
who potentially have much to say about the phenomenology of

our earliest psychological states. These are, respectively, the
mystic and the severely personality disordered, for example, the
psychopath.

The mystic is distinguished by his or her oceanic experiences.
Freud (1932) regarded the oceanic experience to be a residual of
primary narcissism, a well-preserved relic from the architecture
of our earliest mind-state. Approximately 30 percent of a cross
section of American adults claim that they have had oceanic or
near-oceanic experiences (Gallup 1976). (Occasionally, I do hear
from my patients about these transcendental, spiritual, quasi-
sensible, other-worldly, or what-have-you conditions described
so well by William James in "The Reality of the Unseen" [1902].)
Why are some people capable of such states, while others are
completely oblivious to them?

It will not do to maintain that all those who have oceanic
awarenesses are simply children who have not grown up, or
crazy, or narcissistically disturbed, or regressed, etc., as is the
tendency of the more sober-minded among us. When Romain
Rolland spoke of his "oceanic" experiences to Freud, or Bruno
Walter talked of being transported from reality by "heavenly
glory" (see Johnson) or Bellow (1976) offered that "light [is] the
outer garment of God," they did so in full possession of their
extraordinary faculties. We must conclude, I believe, that for
some—a large minority—there remains throughout life a special
pull or attraction from the "deep well of all object-directed libidinal and aggressive strivings" (Jacobson 1964, p. 18). This drawing
power is not due to a defect in ego formation but rather is a
function of the intensity of the original state. As Emerson (1850)
said of the great Swedish mystic Swedenborg, "With a force of
many men, he could never break the umbilical cord which held
him to nature" (p. 136).

Perhaps it is significant that some of my patients who have
improved greatly during the course of their intensive psychotherapy or psychoanalysis have also come to know the oceanic
state or have at least begun to experience some of its lappings on
their psychological shores. As they have derepressed their sexuality and have begun to feel better about themselves, they have

also gotten in touch with what, for lack of a better word, might be called a "spiritual" sense of things.

In stark contrast to those who have or develop an oceanic awareness are the severely personality-disordered individuals. These "subtly constructed reflex machine[s]" (Cleckley 1941, p. 259) show an impenetrable coldness, an absence of self, an incapacity for even plain everyday feelings that suggests that the "deep well" is dry. These troubled and troublesome persons stagger through life by virtue of their instinct-laden autonomous ego functions without the complement of object ego (Horton 1976a, 1976b, 1976c, 1977; Horton et al. 1974).

Individual differences in primary narcissism, particularly with respect to the existence of an oceanic state, may therefore contribute greatly to differential transitional capacities. For example David Copperfield's extraordinary transitional proclivities were intimately bound up, not only with an intense maternal primary process presence, but also with an underlying and correlative readiness for oceanic awarenesses.

The orienting function of the first transitional object

Though transitional objects are orienting at all stages of life, nowhere is this clearer than during the first years of childhood. Of course, the infant is not oriented in the customary sense of person, place, and time or in the more specialized senses of being able to distinguish right from left or construct block designs. Yet, we do not ordinarily say that the infant is "disoriented." This is because the proper or first-degree orientation for the infant is interpersonal and particularly to the mother. I suggested earlier that this internalization is so essential and basic that it may be the product of "imprinting." The mother is, in a sense, the infant's world. As Spitz (1965) has said: "From the beginning of life it is the mother, the human partner of the child, who mediates every perception, every action, every insight, every knowledge" (p. 101).

The child is able to leave the mother's bosom when he or she can find something of her nurturance in the external world. This is the second degree of object orientation—to be able to find objects resonant with the soothing maternal primary process presence. Without the ability to do this the world is, after a brief period of exploration, frighteningly foreign.

Considering the fact that nonhuman primates also show capacity for transitional relatedness, it is probably not too far afield to suggest that nature has conferred the human capacity for transitional relatedness as a distinct biologically rooted phenomenon. Transitional relatedness permits exploration of the external world and eventual separation from the mother and her surrogates. As the child develops the ability to reliably conjure up the mother's soothing qualities vis-à-vis inanimate objects, other people, even ideas, he has a compass and convoy to the unfamiliar, strange, and challenging.

The neurological root of transitional relatedness was explored in an earlier article (Horton 1976a, 1976c). The developmental independence of early-life transitional relatedness from verbal-symbolic growth (usually a function of the left hemisphere), its orienting function, its role in creative activities, and its primary process components suggest that it may have principally nondominant parietal lobe and cerebellar correlates.

Psychopathology connected with distortions in transitional object usage during infancy

This is the stage at which those destined to be personality disordered go astray (Horton, 1976a, 1976b, 1976c, 1977; Horton et al. 1974). I am referring here to personality disorder as a well-defined clinical syndrome and not merely as an aspect of character pathology as the psychoanalyst might think of it. The personality-disordered patient in the DSM II sense is a very disturbed person who would never lie on the couch. Rather than creating abiding soothing presences that provide a healthy basis for later object relations, these unfortunate individuals create either no presences or very rudimentary ones, or even hostile ones which thrive on self-hatred and its projections. Anyone who has worked closely with these patients in military settings and prisons, or in clinics where they may be compelled by the law to seek treatment, knows well the basic emptiness and negativism with respect to object relations that proves to be so resistant to change. How tragically different this is from the normal development of a reliable sense of the soothing, loving One.

Some cases diagnosed "borderline syndrome" may take root in the latter part of this stage. Arkema (1981) had described the rigid, regressive, and maladaptive transitional relatedness exhibited by forty-five adult and adolescent borderline syndrome patients admitted to a private psychiatric hospital. All of these patients readily described their intense attachment to transitional objects both tangible and intangible. The intensity and often highly symbolic nature of the transitional relatedness shown by these patients suggests that they were further along the object relations continuum than those patients who would experience a developmental disturbance during the first stage.

However, there is a group—evidently a small minority—of borderline syndrome patients whose central object relations disturbance may begin during the first year or two of life. At the Philadelphia Naval Hospital, I studied informally several well-defined borderline syndrome patients diagnosed according to the criteria of Grinker, Werble, and Drye (1968). These exceptionally impulsive patients, who showed intense, usually negative, affect and who relied strongly on the mechanism of splitting, gave a history of fleeting transitional relatedness. They may have had a special object for a brief period of time as a child. Or they may have related transitionally in a chaotic and short-lived manner to a series of other people. More primitive, hostile, and aggressive than the patients Arkema describes, they fall developmentally somewhere between the personality-disordered and the more typical borderline syndrome patient. Systematic research is needed to clarify these hypothesized distinctions.

Ages two to six

Whereas the previous stage included one main object-related challenge for the child to overcome—that is, weaning from the

all-absorbing symbiosis and simultaneous differentiation and con-
solidation of the internal psychological representation of the
soothing mother—this stage provides several object-related
challenges. The child must learn to give up the illusion of the
mother as his or her sole possession. The bourgeoning instinctual
yearnings are capped and the incest barrier erected. Male children begin to cope with their fears of losing their favorite toy,
while female children must come to understand that a cleft is not
necessarily the absence of something. Experimentation with objects both internal and external to find those that are congruent
with the soothing maternal primary process presence begins in
earnest.

The transitional object at this stage usually but not always re-
tains obvious qualities as a soother. The colorful stuffed animal is
cuddly, gives warmth, and has a soft glow in its eyes and a pleasing smile. Smell and taste often remain important. However,
since the choice of the object is a function of a new ego organization, the association with or symbolism of the nurturant mother or
the way in which it functions as a soother may be less obvious and
require analysis. For example, it is not readily apparent why the
small child would choose a symbol of a dangerous animal—bear,
lion, tiger, large dog, etc.—as a soother or how it reminds the
child of the nurturant mother.

Before examining this puzzling fact, it must also be emphasized
that there are virtually an infinite number of potential soothers
available to children (unless, of course, the child comes from
extreme poverty and deprivation). The *child* ultimately decides
whether or which one he or she will use. This is strikingly apparent when the youngster throws all of the elaborate stuffed animals
and blankets out of the bed and chooses humble bits of soft paper
diaper or a piece of fuzz with which to stroke his lips. Or, as
described earlier, the child may prefer an imaginary companion
or other intangible.

Sometimes physical texture virtually disappears at this stage as
a determinant of transitional object choice. The connection between the object chosen and the nurturant breast-mother is hard
to make at first glance if the former is something like an orna-
mental china lion (see Freud 1900, p. 190). The soothing effect

due to the texture of porcelain ware would seem to be quite muted in comparison with the stuffed animal or silky edge of the blanket. The china lion may be soothingly colorful and smooth, yet it also represents a ferocious beast. A careful, painstaking analysis of subtle and complicated attachments may be necessary to identify the existence of transitional relatedness. This should not surprise us since, as Arlow (1964) has pointed out, the harmonious integration of various intrapsychic forces makes it "most difficult, if not impossible, to demarcate the limits of the component structures of the mind" (p. 12).

Taking the choice of teddy bear or stuffed lion or other paradoxical soother as examples to analyze, we may recall that, according to Freud, there are many ways in which the dangerous animal symbol can function: as unacceptable impulse (1900, p. 140); dreaded father (1900, p. 410); invective (1900, pp. 405–6); sibling (1900, p. 357); reminder of castration or the threat of such (1909, p. 34); and—most important for the present purpose—as the mother (1909).* The oedipal-aged child, when he or she uses the dangerous animal symbol as a transitional object, is able to bring all of these determinants together in a *soothing* final common pathway. The angry, dangerous, and overly stimulating elements of the oedipal conflict are suppressed and repressed in favor of the maternal determinant.

An example of the existence of a maternal core in such an attachment is given by an oedipally conflicted four-year-old boy who had taken "Big Foot," a giant, hairy, frightening monster on a popular children's television program, into the intermediate area of experience. This boy "love[d] monsters" and once burst in on his bathing mother to exclaim: "Hey mom, your gina [vagina] looks like Big Foot!"

That a mobile concrete object could be a disguised representation of the mother for the modern child is not surprising, especially if we take into account certain paleoanthropologic evidence: Cro-Magnon man worshiped a mother goddess in the form of an artifact sculptured in stone and animal horn (Modell 1968).

* Freud showed how the giraffe's neck—the giraffe probably having been a transitional object for Little Hans before it became a phobic object (p. 33)—was connected in Little Hans's mind with his mother.

Teddy bears, monsters, and similar things may be understood as modern-day versions of these "Venuses" dating back 15,000 years.

Other examples of the maternal source of more covert ("closet") transitional relatedness are the following. A four-year-old boy almost always entered his nursery school with a "toy" from home. A typical incident concerned his bringing a Viewmaster to class. His mother stood patiently at the door of the nursery school while he hung up his coat and proceeded to set up the machine. After the children had gathered around him and he had their rapt attention, his mother quietly slipped out. He showed the pictures for a few minutes and then carefully put the Viewmaster away and joined in other activities. Over the course of the year, he brought a diversity of things (catapult game, Frankenstein mask, etc.) to facilitate his daily entrance. Some of the teachers found his behavior annoying, interpreting it as "attention seeking" or his wanting to be the "center of attention." However, it was clear that the Viewmaster and other such objects had the main function of helping him to separate from his mother while still retaining a sense of her presence and facilitating his adaptation to a conflictual and challenging situation. These objects, more than toys or attention getters, were transitional objects. (Of course, according to the principle of multiple function—the undertaking of action that leads to simultaneous satisfaction of demands from several sources—there may have been, and undoubtedly were, other complementary determinants.)

Similarly, Mahler (1975) described a little girl's nursery school coatroom behavior:

> ... she went to the cubby room to touch her mother's and her
> own outer garments that hung there...; the cubby room...
> served as a kind of transitional space or room—transi-
> tional between the toddler room where the children were
> supposed to be without the mothers and the infant room
> where the mothers stayed. The touching of the clothes in
> Wendy's case seemed to reflect some sort of symbolic "re-
> fueling." Following this "refueling" episode Wendy was then
> able to play comparatively independently from her mother for

a while. She was even able to join the other children in the toddler room who were playing with play dough. [P. 165]

Thus far I have emphasized transitional object choice as a by-product of an ever-changing ego organization. The relationship is reciprocal. Indeed, "the ability to experience in the transitional mode is *essential* for optimal ego development..." (Coppolillo 1976, p. 38; italics added). Early ego growth is a function of the interplay between, in part, the instinctual drives and the forces of external reality. The transitional or intermediate area of experience is "an ideal arena in which the ego can mix these two tides of stimuli" (p. 38).

The bear can represent all of the elements of oedipal conflict—the dreaded and yearned-for father and mother, exciting but forbidden genital and pregenital sexuality, castration fear, penis envy, hostility, and rivalrous siblings. The immobile teddy bear is a virtual stage production company for the gratifying enactment of the conflict. Referring to Rapaport's concept of the autonomies of the ego (from the id and external reality), Coppolillo (1976) says: "To have an object available in this way is invaluable for the ego because it affords it a great degree of control. If the drive component becomes too imperative, the ego can cathect the realistic qualities of the object. If, conversely, the reality becomes too oppressive or boring, more of the inner world of wishes is permitted into awareness" (p. 42).

The percentage of normal children who use transitional objects

Although Winnicott claimed that transitional object usage was virtually universal, beginning at four to twelve months of age, and Bak (1974) has said that "there is a fair consensus that it is a nearly universal and healthy phenomenon in infancy," many studies involving direct observations of children have reported that at least a sizable minority show no transitional object attachment (Busch et al. 1978). An extreme was Gaddini's (1975) finding that 95 percent of a rural Italian group failed to develop a transitional object. More recently, Boniface et al. (1979) reported that only 16 percent of normal three-year-olds had "attachment objects." Anglo-Saxon children appear to use transitional objects more than members of other cultural groups that have been surveyed (Hong 1978).

Clearly, we must distinguish between *manifest* and *covert* transitional relatedness. Winnicott was driving at this when he separated transitional objects and phenomena. The transitional "phenomenon" was introduced, I think, to take into account the hard-to-identify instances of transitional relatedness. An excessively concretistic approach to the study of transitional relatedness—an overemphasis on the tangible, inanimate object—will lead to many false negatives for transitional relatedness and make it appear to be a cultural fad, or Anglo-Saxon idiosyncrasy, rather than a manifestation of the important ego function that it is.

To be considered are instances of covert (or "closet") transitional relatedness. An example is the following:

A twenty-eight-year-old nurse was, at first, unable to recall attachment in childhood to treasured soothers such as stuffed animals or blankets. A few weeks later, after mulling the question over a bit, she reported that, when she was around three to five years of age, she used to live with her grandmother and did have a favorite soother. She liked to slip into her grandmother's room and to listen to the latter's music box while stroking her cheek with a powder puff. As far as she knew, she was the only person aware of this activity. She wondered whether or not it might be analogous to having a blanket or stuffed animal.

We can be sure that in many incidence studies of transitional relatedness, such unstereotypical examples do not find their way into the data. Also, it is to be remembered that the mother herself (Winnicott 1953) and other people become transitional objects.

In addition to considering the potentialities for unrecognized instances of transitional object usage, we must distinguish more clearly between the *capacity* and the *ability* for transitional relatedness. The child who clutches the teddy bear shows both

capacity and ability for transitional relatedness. The child who
shows no such attachment may lack the ability (or the attachment
may be covert). This does not necessarily mean that he lacks the
capacity.

The mother who permits, encourages, or demands that the
child cling to her is not fostering his ability for attachment to
extramaternal objects that would be obvious to the researcher
bent on collecting statistics. Coppolillo (1967) described a depressed mother's interference with her child's development of his
transitional capacities. Such cases are not hard to find now that
we have been alerted to their existence:

> A thirty-year-old man could recall no attachments early in life
> to inanimate soothers. However, in the present, he showed
> transitional object relationships with other persons, including
> his wife and me. His recollections of early childhood ex-
> plained this discrepancy. He had been reared, until adoles-
> cence, in the absence of his father due, in part, to economic
> reasons. His depressed and lonely mother held him closely to
> her, well into latency, essentially infantilizing him with exces-
> sive interest in his bodily functioning. An important part of his
> treatment was the working through and resolution of a per-
> sisting sense of symbiotic and regressive transitional related-
> ness to his deceased mother. His mother had kept his libidinal
> cathexes focused on herself and, as an alternative, on his own
> body, to the detriment of the wider world of relationship pos-
> sibilities. He had developed little interest in objects that might
> stand for his mother in her absence since she, and her ap-
> pointed substitute, the patient's body, were continuously, ab-
> sorbingly, and imperiously present.

I had worked with the patient for approximately 125 hours before
being able to arrive at the formulation that the patient's body was
an early transitional object for him. What I wish to emphasize
with this example is that observations of nursery school children,
interviews of their mothers, questionnaires, and the like cannot
possibly tap into the transitional realities of cases such as these.

We have also to consider the age-of-onset issue. If one defines
transitional relatedness as a phenomenon restricted to the early

pre-oedipal years, one need go no further. But what then do we
say about the six-year-old who takes up a stuffed animal or blanket for the first time? I have witnessed the later onset of transitional relatedness often enough to be cautious about gener-
alizations regarding the percentage of normal children who use or
do not use them. An example follows from my work with a
personality-disordered boy.

A 9-year-old boy, the second of three siblings, was brought
by his mother for psychiatric evaluation with the chief complaint, "We can't get him to go along with what we want."
The incident resulting in referral was his threatening his older
brother with a knife. His mother reported that "he always
seemed to have a mean streak, was easily upset, and would
have to get even for anything that was done to him." He
had no history of transitional relatedness.

From the outset he sought to structure the hour's activities
as completely and rigidly as possible. After many sessions
during which he verbalized very little about himself, his family, school, or friends, I introduced, with some initial difficulty, a teddy bear and two dolls for play. He named the
teddy bear Bruce and the two dolls Sam and Blackie. The patient spoke for Bruce, and I spoke for the dolls.

Bruce hit the dolls often. When they protested the hurt, he
replied, "I have no feelings. I'm super. See, I can fly and twist
my arms and legs in all directions." He challenged the dolls to
hit him to prove that he had no feelings of hurt. They refused,
stating that they had no desire to hit him. He persisted:
"Come on! Hit me! I'll show you. Come on, I don't mind. Hit
me." Sam demurred, asking him what it was like to be without feelings of pain. He said it was good, that without such
feelings he could be super. He denigrated human beings, especially women, as weak because they had feelings. Sam and
Blackie stated that they liked being filled with feelings of all
kinds, that feelings made life rich. Bruce replied anxiously,
"But, I'm stronger—see, I can turn my head all the way
around." Blackie said, "It's good that you are strong. But I
wouldn't trade my feelings just to be strong." Bruce then revealed that he was a "robot bear from outer space" and that it
was impossible for him to have feelings.

In a subsequent session, Sam offered to hug Bruce to help

him learn about human feelings. The patient reacted with
acute agitation, put Bruce down, and said, "I don't like that
hugging stuff." Returning to play, he mercilessly pummeled
the dolls until they had to retreat from reach. They resumed
play only on the condition that he not hit them. He broke his
promise, however, and again forced the dolls to retreat under
a barrage of blows. Finally, after several broken promises, the
dolls withdrew and stated that they would not return that day.
Bruce begged them to come back. They hesitated. He offered,
"If you come back, I'll even hug you."

During the ensuing week, the patient suffered for several
days from a headache that reached its apex on the day of the
session. At the beginning of the therapy hour *he* eagerly initiated play with Bruce and the dolls. Bruce informed the dolls
that he was the "old Bruce's twin brother." He explained that
he had come in Bruce's place because Bruce was away seeing
a "computer doctor." The doctor would fix Bruce so that
"He would have feelings too." After a while the old Bruce
reappeared and offered to hug the dolls as proof of his cure.
The headache remitted but the "fixed" Bruce was worried. In
order to be cured, he had had to give up his super strength.
He was now merely strong. At home, improvements were
noticed: he had begun snuggling up to his parents on the
couch; he had discovered his siblings and had begun playing
with them. His mother—an emotionally timid woman—was
bewildered by his accusation, "You don't love me." The social worker explored ways in which the parents, especially the
mother, might show more emotional accessibility and initia-
tive. She was encouraged, for example, to kiss the patient
goodnight even if he did not ask. After 6 months of therapy
the attacks on the dolls had become infrequent. Bruce now
protected the dolls from the school principal, creatures from
outer space, and other menacing figures. The patient's growing fondness for Bruce and the dolls was paralleled by sub-
stantial improvement in his relationships at home, at school,
with peers, and with me. [A follow-up interview, two years
after therapy was completed, showed sustained improvement.]*

* From P. C. Horton, "The Psychological Treatment of Personality Disorder,"
American Journal of Psychiatry, vol 133, pp. 262–65, 1976. Copyright 1976, the
American Psychiatric Association. Reprinted by permission.

Thus, all things considered, it is difficult to know the true incidence of childhood transitional object usage. It is probably well in excess of 90 percent. My own published (Horton et al. 1974) and unpublished surveys of adults asked to recall childhood attachments show better than nine out of ten children having exhibited the ability. Indeed, asking adults about their childhood soothers is probably a more accurate way of assessing the incidence of childhood attachment since: (1) true transitional objects are not forgotten or their memory repressed; (2) with this procedure, we depend neither on the limited definitional imagination of the researcher nor on the observational limitations inherent in attempting to detect attachment to intangibles on the part of preverbal children; and (3) it should be much easier to discriminate between soothers and fetishes (Greenacre 1969; Bak 1974), since the former are recalled with ease and without embarrassment.

Actually, we probably should not be surprised to learn that the capacity for transitional relatedness is virtually ubiquitous in normal persons: Even infant chimpanzees "raised in nurseries under conditions similar to those for human infants, develop transitional object relationships identical with those seen in human infants" (Kollar 1972).

Distortions in transitional object usage at this stage

Future schizophrenically disturbed patients will often first give evidence of their later disturbance during this stage by clinging regressively to the blanket or some other tangible soother and by not moving on to or adding more complicated or subtle objects (Horton 1977). There is a congruity between this observation and one reported by Bak (1974): "'It is not rare for deteriorated schizophrenics, after decades of institutionalizations, to carry a bag with (for us) worthless pieces of leather, buttons, etc.—lost remnants of object relationships. It is also possible that the word salad and verbigeration of old schizophrenics contain some elements of infantile "transitional babbling"'" (personal communication, Walter A. Stewart)."

Future personality-disordered persons who have not invested
an object representative of the symbiosis will not, of course, find
any special objects whatever.

Several authors have described connections between direct observations of childhood psychopathology and disturbances in relation to transitional object usage. Among these are reports of
studies of institutionalized children: "Although dolls and stuffed
animals were available, in no instance did an institutional infant
develop an attachment to a specific toy which became a comforter
or friend. There were no transitional objects as described by
Winnicott (1953)" (Provence et al. 1961). Others have made
similar connections (Provence et al. 1962; Pavenstedt 1967). In
these studies, severe developmental disturbances appear to precede the inability to experience transitional relatedness.

In other studies involving direct observations of children, the
reciprocal relationship between the failure to use transitional objects and emotional disturbance is more transparent. For example, Kris (1962) reports on a disturbed three-year-old as follows:

> In Anne's development the low investment of the comfort
> situation, the inadequate structure of the experience with the
> mother, seems to be paralleled by her inability to take interest
> in toys or to play with inanimate objects which might sub-
> stitute for the human object, a retardation which will last for a
> long time. It will persist in the inability to perform in-
> dependent problem solving. The test situation in which this
> problem solving is first studied is one in which a toy is hidden
> by a cloth or screen [in the last quarter of the first year]. The
> child is to retrieve the toy. The observation of Anne and of
> institutional children gives the impression that at first the hid-
> den toy is not important enough to be recovered. Soon, how-
> ever, it appears that initiative to evaluate the situation, the
> activity necessary to retrieve the toy, is blocked: a deficit in
> thinking seems to be operating.

Escalona's (1963) observations are also supportive of the clinical
importance of a derailment of the transitional developmental line.
She shows that the child who is unresponsive to inanimate objects
may also resist social stimulation—a capacity (or incapacity) that

may be "perceived as antagonism and resistance by the social environment" (p. 225). Similarly, Stevenson (1954, p. 207) observed: " . . . there are cases where one feels that a conspicuous lack of any transitional object may be an indication of a deviation away from the normal, whether it be toward an extreme of dependence on or independence from the mother."

Latency

At age eight David Copperfield's "only and constant comfort" were the books bequeathed to him by his mother. As tangible, physical objects—reliable representatives of external reality, to use Coppolillo's (1976) words—they are taken into the intermediate area of experience between "me and not-me," between mother and self. In this sense, he related to the books like an infant to its blanket. Of course, the books are not cuddly and soft like the blanket or stuffed animal and, therefore, lack the textural maternal dimension.

Latency-aged and even older children very often temporarily regress to the use of tangible, physical soothers. An example is an eleven-year-old girl who, when lonely for her vacationing mother, soothed herself by going to her mother's closet and stroking the latter's bathrobe. The act of stroking the bathrobe reoriented her and gave her the sense of being safely within her mother's purview.

There is another facet of Copperfield's experience in the intermediate area that foreshadows a developmental tendency in the normal use of transitional objects. The books were more than mere concrete objects that were associated with the soothing mother. They also contained words that evoked pleasurable fantasies, stimulated play, and prompted adaptive identification with heroic figures. All of this was accomplished in a soothing final common pathway: The books, more than anything else, relieved his sense of "being daily more and more shut out and alienated from [his] mother."

The infant recalls the mother by stroking the fingers, lips, or cheek with the soft fringe of the blanket. The four-year-old cuddles with the soft teddy bear and, in addition to feeling closer to the mother, achieves a soothing illusion of conflict resolution by controlling the symbolic wild animal. The latency-aged youngster may be relatively little soothed by the physical qualities of the preferred transitional object. The adventure book, for example, is not literally soft and warm. Its agreeableness is essentially intangible, abstract, and symbolic.

At age ten Copperfield showed that he was able to rely exclusively on psychological imagery for the purpose of self-soothing. The concrete object was given up altogether. The "quiet picture [he] had conjured up of [his] mother in her youth and beauty" always "went before [him] and [he] followed." He was "led and sustained" by that "fanciful picture" which "always kept [him] company."

It is possible that Copperfield utilized purely psychological transitional objects much earlier in life. Since the story begins with the eight-year-old boy, we do not know anything definite about his oedipal and pre-oedipal years. The first transitional object that is described is a book. However, it would not be surprising to find that Copperfield had many other precursor objects, some of which may have been as intangible as his fantasy of "mother . . . in her youth and beauty." As I described in the last section, children at around two years of age may begin to speak about abstract transitional imaginary companions.

The following is an example of a latency-aged girl's use of poetry as a transitional object:

> A fifty-five-year-old woman recalled sadly having been given over to her grandparents for rearing when she was seven years old. Her mother was too burdened with younger children to care for her. Psychologically devastated, she turned to poems by Longfellow for soothing. These poems meant so much to her that, even today, she treasures the worn-out poetry book.

Another woman, who was raised in rural Georgia, attended a one-room schoolhouse at the turn of the century. All of the

children, from kindergarten through eighth grade, were required
to memorize poetry. On Fridays each student was asked to recite a
new poem in front of the class. When this woman was eleven
years old her mother suddenly and tragically died. The girl
compensated in various ways, but perhaps very strongly intellectually and transitionally, learning even more poetry than was
required—poetry that in her tenth decade of life she recites at
bedtime, when alone, and when traveling. Lately her eyes have
been failing her, and she says the poems over and over to herself.
One poem in particular—a poem about death that she learned at
age sixteen—has special meaning and solacing value for her. It is
remarkable how much poetry she knows and how it lives in her
from latency.

Pre-adolescent boys often collect things—bottlecaps, napkins
from restaurants, bullet shells, beer cans, stamps, coins, models,
rocks, baseball cards, various trinkets, etc.—that provide some
security, some solacing defense against upsurging sexual, hostile,
aggressive, and sometimes destructive forces. These latency-
age transitional activities may provide an adaptive pathway into
the future—the stamp collector who becomes a successful in-
vestor in stamps, the model builder who becomes an aeronautical
engineer, etc.

While exceptional children cathect intangible soothers—
prayers, poems, imaginary companions, and the like—very early,
and may go back and forth between tangible and abstract objects
or use both during the same period, it is generally the case that
latency-aged children move in the direction of graduating from
tangible soothers to more symbolic ones. Part of this change is a
result of the acquisition of new psychological abilities. Cognitive
growth, the development of the superego, sublimation, and the
appearance of the ego ideal are among important contributing
factors to the transitional mode and content in latency. These
factors and their role vis-à-vis transitional relatedness will be discussed in the chapter on morality. Individual differences in
creativity, intelligence, and temperament interact with family,
class, social, and cultural circumstances to further shape the transitional mode and its contents.

Clinical examples of transitional object usage by
latency-aged children

The following vignettes were contributed by Paul Arkema, M.D.
Dr. Arkema, who is particularly interested in the latency period
and the rich and complex psychological activities that occur in this
usually asymptomatic phase, calls latency "*the* transitional epoch
in life." His case reports support the idea that latency-aged children are actively engaged with transitional objects and that these
vehicles for solace may have considerable clinical significance.

CASE 6

A nine-year-old girl had taken several stuffed animals to a
summer camp. One day at camp, when she was packing her
knapsack for an overnight hike, she had difficulty fitting into
her pack the animals, especially her favorite, a giraffe with a
long neck. A camp counselor said, "You should know they
don't want to go with you." Subsequently, the girl began to
have difficulty sleeping and seemed upset. Not understanding
the change in her, the camp director decided to send her home.

CASE 7

On his eleventh birthday a boy was admitted to a pediatric
service for medical evaluation of repeated urinary tract in-
fections. He stopped eating, occasionally had crying spells,
refused to discuss what he was thinking or feeling, seemed not
to respond to family visits, and showed no interest in toys or
games on the unit. Oldest of six children, and "first grand-
child" to his maternal grandmother, he revealed to the psychiatrist that when he cried he was thinking about his stamp
collection. He described stamps that he and his grandmother,
who died when he was nine, had collected and how they put
them in books. "My mother was always having a baby . . . my
grandmother gave us *warm* cereal. She let us cut the crust off
bread and put as much sugar on cereal as we wanted." The
psychiatrist recommended that the stamp collection be
brought to the boy in the hospital. The parents were skeptical

that it would help because they did not feel the collection had been important to the boy in the past year. However, after the collection was brought to him he brightened up greatly, began to eat, cooperated with all the tests, and engaged the staff and other children in a lively manner about his collection, which he kept next to his bed and added to (with everyone's help) during his stay. Subsequently, he also began to show interest in other toys and games.

CASE 8

A ten-year-old boy was referred for evaluation after a fight in school with another boy his age. He had been called a "fag." The generally passive boy with long blond hair had difficulty reading, especially in front of the class, but did average work and had no evidence of dyslexia. His mother was concerned that he had "changed."

There had been conflict at home around the boy's determination to have a family dog, an old "ugly" boxer with poorly trimmed ears and tail, sleep in his room, particularly on his bed. The boy followed the dog to the shed or to the basement—when it was forbidden in his room at night—in the face of a possible strapping from his father. The parents were puzzled by the boy's attachment to the dog since he had shown relatively little overt interest in the dog before he was seven. They saw his behavior as part of recent "stubbornness." The boy was not very articulate; he merely said it "felt good" to be with the dog—it was "soft, warm, and a good friend."

During the previous two years the mother, who had given him, her youngest child, a lot of attention, was preoccupied with the care of her invalid father. When the latter finally died she became very depressed, and it was six months before she was aware that her son had "changed" and was less responsive to her. She then began to press her husband, a man who worked long hours and did not interact much with the children, to discipline their son. Her emotional unavailability and the father's strictness precipitated his interest in relating to the solacing dog.

CASE 9

An eight-year-old boy, the only child of a divorced woman,
was interviewed because he had told his mother he felt "un-
safe" going on a vacation with her. In the interview he said he
worried that the car might run out of gas or break down. But
he shyly admitted that he would feel safe if he could take his
cash register. His favorite game was playing store. He always
used a cash register in which he stored valuables, including a Batman ring and a key chain his father had given to him. [The
reader may recall Mr. Barkis's special box.]

He was an attractive, well-developed boy, verbal and engaging. The only unusual event in his life had been some soil-
ing for about two months at the time of his parents' separation
when he was five years old. The mother was aware that the
cash register had to be in his bedroom at night and go on trips
with him. She could not remember when the cash register had
become so important, since he had had the toy since age two
or three. She recalled that he had had a "security blanket" until
about age four.

Adolescence

The progression toward the adult years tends to be accompanied
by a loosening of the connection between physical texture and the
soothing that accrues from transitional object usage. The emotionally healthy adolescent does not usually prefer the stuffed
animal or blanket, although these and other relationships to tangible objects are literally more visible than other transitional
manifestations.

This is not to say that earlier modes of transitional relatedness
do not often continue alongside of or even as a part of more
mature modes. For example, the adolescent may still find it
soothing to stroke objects with his or her fingers in the way that
the fringe of the blanket was stroked.

An eighteen-year-old boy with an average intelligence had taken
a teddy bear to bed with him between the ages of two and six.
Under great pressure from his mother he gave up the teddy
bear and substituted a favorite blanket. At puberty he gave up

the blanket—again, under considerable pressure from his
mother—and took up guitar playing. Since he had always liked
to run his fingers lightly over the edges of his silken blanket, it
was not surprising to learn that what he liked best about guitar
playing was "touch." He liked the "softness" that "loosened
up [his] fingers" and the touch that was described variously as
"clear, light, smooth, flexible" or "quick." Predictably, he
preferred "finger picking" to the use of a pick. Although he
had spent thousands of hours developing his skill at guitar
playing, he showed no interest in joining a band or marketing
his talent. He stated that his only goal in playing the instrument was to be "one with [his] guitar." Like Dickens's Mr.
Micawber—and so many other transitionally invested characters in Dickens's novels—he was "never so happy as when he
was busy about something that could never be of any profit to
him" (*Copperfield,* p. 178).

The need "to do it for its own sake," it should be reiterated, is
an identifying feature of activities in the transitional mode: " . . . a
culture's artistic expressions are a psychological necessity for the
individuals in that culture" (Coppolillo 1976). Johan Borg indicates
this experienced necessity in Bergman's *Hour of the Wolf* (1973):
"Nothing is self-evident in what I create—except the compulsion
to create it." Van Gogh gives similar testimony: "Painting is
something in itself" (Heiman 1976). So does Wagner (1892, vol. 1,
p. 48): "The *true artist* finds delight not only in the aim of his
creation, but also in the very process of creation, in the handling
and moulding of his material. The very act of production is to him
a gladsome, satisfying activity: no toil." (The discussion of
Emerson's experience in the transitional mode in the next section
will amplify this point.)

A somewhat immature seventeen-year-old girl with average
intelligence showed a similar development of transitional object
choice to that of the eighteen-year-old boy described above but
with less persistence of the tactile component. She answered the
question "Did you have any special things as a child?" as follows:

My stuffed animals. I dressed them up all the time. I had
about twenty-five of them—they're still in the attic someplace.
I wouldn't let my mother throw them away. I was sorry that
she gave my pink rabbit with the purple ears to the dog. He
chewed it up in a month. It was a gift from my grandmother. . . . I finally narrowed it down to some favorites—a
white poodle that was real cute, a bear and later on, a snake. I
had always had to have one to hold in my right arm at bedtime
until I was about eleven years old. After that a night light was
a replacement for a while. And then [with the onset of pu-
berty] I got interested in music. The music—especially classical
and soft rock—took the place of my stuffed animals. I tried
playing guitar and piano for awhile but wasn't very good at it.
Music is still an escape for me.

Taking these and many other examples of adolescent transitional object usage together, one finds, in addition to the shift in
emphasis from the tangible to the intangible—a diffusion across the
whole cultural field—a trend toward disguise that may make it
impossible to detect the maternal determinant on superficial
examination. It would be unusual, if not pathological, to find in
adolescence the blatantly undefended, soothing maternal primary
process presence described by David Copperfield: a fantasy of
"mother in her youth and beauty."

Part of the reason for this change is that healthy transitional
relatedness helps the adolescent to "achieve resonance and unity
with the culture" and functions as a "drive modulator and
catalyst" for ego development (Coppolillo 1976). The adolescent
is charged with the responsibility of consciously giving up his or
her need for direct maternal nurturance. In whatever way the
preferred transitional object represents the mother, it must do so
with subtlety as exemplified by the graduation from stroking the
nursing mother's hair, to fingering the fringe of the blanket, to
cuddling the stuffed animal, to softly plucking the guitar strings.
The adolescent who clings to the blanket is a "mommy's boy" (or
girl); the adolescent who is an accomplished guitarist is "with it."
Social acceptability of the transitional object is usually paramount

in adolescence and is balanced against the adolescent's "need to
do it for its own sake."

The adult years

The mature transitional object par excellence is the soothing vision. A vision may be defined as a persisting vivid conception, an
object of imaginative contemplation that involves looking at reality from a particular perspective and not others. Schafer (1976)
describes several types of visions—comic, romantic, tragic, and
ironic. If the vision is comic it supports "unqualified hopeful-
ness" and "tidings of joy." A "happy ending," a utopian world,
heaven on earth, and the possibility of eternal rebirth are qualities
associated with the unalloyed comic vision.

The romantic vision conceptualizes life as a "quest" that may
be "perilous, heroic, individualistic." Its destination "combines
some or all of the qualities of mystery, grandeur, sacredness, love
and possession by or fusion with some higher power or principle." Nature is often idealized, and there is "nostalgia for a golden
age," even pursuit of the *earth mother* in her various incarnations.

In contrast, the tragic vision emphasizes the "great dilemmas,
paradoxes, ambiguities, and uncertainties pervading human action and subjective experience. It manifests itself in alertness to
the inescapable dangers, terrors, mysteries, and absurdities of
existence." The ironic vision is closely related to the tragic in its
emphasis of the contradictions, ambiguities, and paradoxes in
life. However, it seeks in addition to establish a salutary
detachment—a mitigation of the seriousness with which one regards the human condition.

The quality of the vision at the beginning of life is, of course,
comic-romantic. The infant with his blanket is seeking an unqualified heaven on earth. However, by the age of three or four
the comic-romantic vision has already been tempered by dimly
perceived tragic elements. The spontaneous substitution of the
stuffed animal for a part of the mother shows that the child is
beginning to consider the possibility that loss in some sense must
be suffered, that there is no immediate turning back and rebirth

into the primal paradise. The ironic makes its first appearance in the child's choice of the symbolically dangerous animal (e.g., the stuffed lion or bear) as a soother. It marks the beginning of the child's ability to seek out and integrate the paradoxical and contradictory. I am not suggesting that the four-year-old's vision is self-reflective or that he can articulate its components. Rather, I am calling attention to the roots of the later, more adult visions in these early conceptions.

Contemplation of an especially well-articulated adult vision will help sensitize us to the less skillfully enunciated, less self-reflective, but more prevalent soothing visions we may find in ourselves, in others, and in our patients. The essays and poems of Ralph Waldo Emerson can be readily understood as expressions of transitional relatedness. Typical of Emerson's writings is the following (Emerson 1954):

> There are days which occur in this climate, at almost any season of the year, wherein the world reaches its perfection; when the air, the heavenly bodies and the earth make a harmony, as if Nature would indulge her offspring; when, in these bleak upper sides of the planet, nothing is to desire that we have heard of the happiest latitudes, and we bask in the shining hours of Florida and Cuba; when everything that has life gives sign of satisfaction, and the cattle that lie on the ground seem to have great and tranquil thoughts. These halcyons may be looked for with a little more assurance in that pure October weather which we distinguish by the name of Indian summer. The day, immeasurably long, sleeps over the broad hills and warm wide fields. To have lived through all its sunny hours, seems longevity enough. The solitary places do not seem quite lonely. At the gates of the forest, the surprised man of the world is forced to leave his city estimates of great and small, wise and foolish. The knapsack of custom falls off his back with the first step he takes into these precincts. Here is sanctity which shames our religions, and reality which discredits our heroes. Here we find Nature to be the circumstance which dwarfs every other circumstance, and judges like a god all men that come to her. We have crept out of our close and crowded houses into the night and morning, and we see what

majestic beauties daily wrap us in their bosom. How willingly
we would escape the barriers which render them compara-
tively impotent, escape the sophistication and second thought,
and suffer nature to entrance us. The tempered light of the
woods is like a perpetual morning, and is stimulating and
heroic. The anciently-reported spells of these places creep on
us. The stems of pines, hemlocks and oaks almost gleam like
iron on the excited eye. The incommunicable trees begin to
persuade us to live with them, and quit our life of solemn
trifles. Here no history, or church, or state is interpolated on
the divine sky and the immortal year. How easily we might
walk onward into the opening landscape, absorbed by new
pictures and by thoughts fast succeeding each other, until by
degrees the recollection of home was crowded out of mind, all
memory obliterated by the tyranny of the present, and we
were led in triumph by nature. . . . These enchantments are
medicinal, they sober and heal us. These are plain pleasures,
kindly and native to us.

Readers will, of course, vary in their reactions to such statements. Some may find in Emerson's essays the "strange, rapt
music which is easier to hear than to explain" (Van Doren 1975).
Others may find a repellent incomprehensibleness, denseness, an
unction, a callowness that is not redeemed by philosophical
perspicacity. Whatever one's personal reactions, I invite the
reader to see what may be discovered about the presence of a
transitional mode of experience and expression without challenging the validity of its content.

It is clear, I think, that Emerson's description of the medicinal
enchantments that "sober and heal us," those "plain pleasures"
that are "kindly and native," was intended to soothe the reader
(and perhaps Emerson himself) through the invocation of images
of *mother* earth. In support of this are references to nature's
harmonies, *her* halcyons, *her* sanctity, *her* tempered but stimulating light, and *her* "majestic beauties that wrap us in their bosom."
Elsewhere in *Nature* we find the "secret promises" and "soft
glances," the "umbilical cord" that is not cut (p. 19), the "force
of heaven that soothes us to wiser convictions," the "invisible
spiritual reality" that is the "root of all cultural and social in-

stitutions'' (p. 23), the ''soothing dreams'' and the necessity of staying at home with the ''internal ocean'' (p. 64). Thus, there is, in effect, an appeal—not too far removed from con-sciousness—by Emerson to the ''felt presence,'' to the libidi-nal tie to the soothing nurturant breast-mother that has never been entirely given up at unconscious levels by the normal adult.

Emerson articulated many of the qualities of what has come to be called the transitional mode. In a general way, he saw nature and its contents as a ''system in transition'' (p. 16) and endorsed physical, spiritual, and psychological evolution. He spoke of the ubiquity of ''transformational'' processes, as in ''Nature is the in-carnation of a thought, and turns to thought again, as ice becomes water and gas'' (p. 23). He was one of the earliest structural/ego psychologists:

> Now we learn what patient periods must round themselves
> before the rock is formed; then before the rock is broken, and
> the first lichen race has disintegrated the thinnest external
> plate into soil, and opened the door for the remote Flora,
> Fauna, Ceres and Pomona to come in. How far off is the trilo-
> bite! how far the quadruped! how inconceivably remote is
> man! All duly arrive, and then race after race of men. It is a
> long way from granite to oyster; farther yet to Plato and the
> preaching of the immortality of the soul. . . . Plants are the
> young of the world, vessels of health and vigor; but they
> *grope ever upward toward consciousness.* [P. 16; italics
> added]

Throughout his essays we find an emphasis on the evolution of *awareness*.

Like Winnicott, Emerson saw the importance of illusion and expressed this pithily in many ways such as the following: ''The difference between landscape and landscape is small, but there is great difference in the beholders'' (p. 14). His essay, ''Illu-sions,'' was an erudite analysis of the subject. In fact, he per-ceived *lifelong* transformational processes in illusion formation:

> I find men victims of illusion in all parts of life. Children,
> youths, adults and old men, all are led by one bauble or
> another. . . . There are as many pillows of illusion as flakes in a

snow storm. We wake from one dream into another dream. The toys to be sure are various, and are graduated in refinement to the quality of the dupe. The intellectual man requires a fine bait; the sots are easily amused. But everybody is drugged with his own frenzy, and the pageant marches at all hours, with music and banner and badge. [Van Doren 1975, p. 228]

Emerson said that he could not go back to toys, that he had "grown expensive and sophisticated" (Emerson 1954, p. 13). However, he was never so sophisticated as to give up the nurturant breast-mother: "Women, more than all, are the element and kingdom of illusion" (Van Doren 1975, p. 229).

It is clear, too, that he saw soothing illusion formation as occurring in what Winnicott (1953) labeled the "intermediate area": "The blue zenith is the point in which romance and reality meet (p. 12); and "In every landscape the point of astonishment is the meeting of the sky and earth" (p. 14).

Summarizing, the essays of Emerson, of which *Nature* may be taken as typical, are manifestations of the transitional mode. They reflect, in their inception, all of the elements of transitional experience—maternal imagery, self-object merger, illusion formation, the transition from one level of consciousness to another, and soothing experience in the intermediate area.

The effect of Emerson's essays has also been transitional for generations of readers:

A thirty-five-year-old attorney and former minister recalled having been attached to several of Emerson's essays during the transition from high school to college, from late adolescence to young adulthood. Although he was unable to re-collect the details of the essays, he remembered their having been helpfully soothing to him when he was struggling with issues of separation from his parental home.

Let us look at additional examples of adult transitional relatedness on the part of individuals less distinguished than Emerson:

A thirty-year-old civil servant was attached to a panda bear between the ages of one and eight. He stated: "My bear really got beaten up. It lost its eyes and was ripped open many times. Each time my mother would sew it back together until finally she threw it away. She didn't tell me that she was going to do that and when I found it in the trash I was shocked. I retrieved it and hid it in the basement. She finally found it again and explained to me that I was too old to have a Teddy and that it was worn out anyway." In high school he played several musical instruments and fantasized that he would find a "tall, thin beautiful blond" as a groupie. At age twenty-five, during a period of marital crisis, he began composing songs. The lyrics he devised—"I felt like a part of you, I wonder if I'll miss you, happiness is just an illusion," etc., and his associations to them support the conclusion that he related to his wife as a transitional object. He said: "It's always been important to me to have a woman in my life; the thought of being alone is scarey." He also tended to exploit his wife in the manner of a small child who tosses his teddy in the corner when not in need of soothing. Fortunately, this pattern was modulated by his awareness of the "selfish" and "immature" quality of the behavior. He did, however, let himself be more ruthless with his musical compositions, creating and treasuring them for a while, and then filing or destroying them. The connection between his adult transitional object behavior and his mother was clear. He said: "There was always something soothing about discussing things with my mother. In a way I feel that she still is controlling my thoughts." This sense of her "still controlling [his] thoughts" even though deceased is best interpreted as an instance of the existence and force of the maternal primary process presence.

A forty-year-old humanities professor recalled a series of transitional objects the first of which was a teddy bear that he began using at age two. This lasted until age seven, when it was lost in moving. He also had several blankets in succession. The first blanket became the lining of the second, which in turn became the lining of the third. His mother finally made him give up the tattered remains when he was eleven years old. He also became very interested in music and could recall special tunes that he had heard before the age of five. He liked to play records on the phonograph when his parents were out for the evening and found this either very exciting or

soothing. At age nine he had his first mystical experience.
This occurred at a very stressful time in his parents' life when
his depressed mother was emotionally unavailable to him. The
specific incident that led up to the mystical experience was
his mother's insensitive rebuff when he had hoped that she
would comfort him. Distressed and feeling guilty, he went to
his room and began to pray. (This was an understandable
alternative to direct maternal soothing since his mother had
taught him to pray when he was four or five years old.) As he
prayerfully asked for forgiveness for whatever it was that he
had done to create the rift between himself and his parents, he
suddenly found himself within the purview of the most awe-
somely peaceful presence he had ever known. After this mystical experience he felt completely forgiven and, for the first
time, was clear about the meaning of the biblical injunction
against making a "graven image." He interpreted this to mean
that he should not "idolize" his exceptional parents—as had
been his tendency—but should see them against the backdrop
of the larger sense of things he had discovered in the mystical
state. Indeed, beginning with that experience, he now felt that
he had two sets of parents—one earthly and one heavenly.
During his teens he became a musician and developed soothing fantasies of the perfect woman—fantasies modeled on several real-life movie stars. He anticipated wooing his ideal mate
through musical brilliance. Additional mystical experiences
were stimulated by a series of family tragedies and his separation from home. In college he majored in philosophy. He was
repelled by the existentialists, who seemed to find only emptiness and "nausea" in their inner being; he had never known
such an experience and concluded that the existentialist view-
point suffered from emotional superficiality. He found the
"analytic" philosophies to be "tedious, lacking in orientation,
and lifeless" and eventually decided on the humanities as a
vocation since they offered greater play to his imaginative
capacities than the logical positivism that was dominant in his
academic circle. A tense, perfectionistic, and temperamental
man, he came to find certain kinds of music to be the most
reliable source of soothing. Many of his favorite compositions
evoked the special sense of peace that he had found in each
mystical state.

A forty-eight-year-old mother of eight had had many dolls to which she had been strongly attached as a child. She had kept some of them stored away even until the present time. Overt attachment to dolls gave way in her early teens to artistic expression, which she found to be very solacing. As an adult she shifted the focus of her transitional relatedness to her children. The birth of each child was eagerly awaited by her. Each became a central transitional object until the arrival of the next child. The appearance of oedipal conflicts and blatantly expressed sexual wishes by each child made her anxious and desirous of another infant. Under stress she often turned to her children for soothing. She delighted in reading children's stories to them and sharing their contentment. Occasionally she projected her own needs and offered soothing to her children when none was warranted. Following a hysterectomy and a reactive depression of six months' duration, she rehabilitated herself by taking care of a succession of welfare babies. This activity eventually gave way to investment in grandchildren.

The loss of the transitional ability

The progressive and regressive uses of transitional relatedness have been presented. Another possible outcome is the temporary or permanent loss of the ability itself. For the religious person this may be augured by "loss of faith." The author's interest in writing and the composer's desire to create may wane. The husband or wife may no longer find the spouse to be exciting, etc. Among the causes are a wearing out of the soothing maternal primary process presence, severe disillusionment, the upsurgence of dominating instinctual aims, and the development of defective ego ideals.

The most impressionistically conceived of these causes is the wearing out of the soothing maternal primary process presence. This occurs at midlife and beyond. Subjectively, the end product is like a "light [having] gone out" or the growing awareness of an "inner void." Experientially, it is the opposite of the mystical state wherein one may see an intensified inner light, or of a near-death experience that leads to a sense of union with loved ones, especially with the mother (Grof and Halifax 1968). The death of the actual mother may initiate a subtle and gradual or dramatic and precipitous decline in the sensitivity to potential transitional objects. For others, a chronic lack of success in finding objects resonant with the soothing maternal primary process presence is crucial. And for still others, there is satiation effect—the richness of life exceeds the psychological complexity of the soothing maternal primary process presence, resulting in a paradoxical boredom.

Perhaps one measure of mental health is the sense that, if one could live life many times over, there would still exist unrealized possibilities for gratifying psychological union with things external to the self. (The reader may recall the remarks of the dying but youthfully resilient Jean-Christophe regarding the next life.)

Comments on this wearing-out process must necessarily be somewhat vague. The main reason is that degeneration of the transitional capacity—if it exists as I hypothesize—proceeds much like aging of the physical body. Although we cannot detect it from month to month, or even over a year or two, it is unequivocally clear after a decade.*

Severe disillusionment leading to temporary loss of the transitional ability is more discrete and easier to describe. Many sailors and marines were subjected to aggressive disillusionment in Viet Nam. Some of those who became psychiatric casualties were unable to recover their ability to cathect the "mission" even with psychiatric hospitalization. Others, if sent home to their mothers for a few weeks, were able to return successfully to active duty. We psychiatrists labeled the mothers "primary therapists." Using Mahler's term, they "refueled" their sons and made it possible for them to recathect soothing illusions about some aspect of the military.

Scrooge, in Dickens's *A Christmas Carol*, was not so fortunate.

---

* In *Back to Methuselah*, George Bernard Shaw had an elder statesman suggest that the length of an ordinary lifetime, say seventy or eighty years, was only long enough for a person to be initiated into the complexities of government. If this is true for politics, it certainly is true for meaningful research into matters of the mind!

It took him nearly a lifetime to recover his ability for experience in the transitional mode. When the elderly Scrooge, whose "master-passion" is "gain," is visited by the Ghost of Christmas Past, he is transported back to childhood. There we learn some important things about the genesis of Scrooge's "odious, stingy, hard and unfeeling" character. Little Fan, Scrooge's beloved younger sister, indicates that their father has been cruel to Scrooge and has sent him away to a boardinghouse. Profoundly lonely, he is treated with "ferocious condescension" by the schoolmaster. The whereabouts of Scrooge's mother are not made known, and it is implied that she has died.

In response to his separation from home, the youthful Scrooge, like the youthful Copperfield, finds transitional relief in books:

> They went, the Ghost and Scrooge, across the hall, to a door at the back of the house. It opened before them, and disclosed a long, bare melancholy room, made barer still by lines of plain deal forms and desks. At one of these a lonely boy was reading near a feeble fire; and Scrooge sat down upon a form, and wept to see his poor forgotten self as he used to be. . . .
>
> The Spirit touched him on the arm, and pointed to his younger self, intent upon his reading. Suddenly a man, in foreign garments: wonderfully real and distinct to look at: stood outside the window, with an axe stuck in his belt, and leading an ass laden with wood by the bridle.
>
> "Why, it's Ali Baba!" Scrooge exclaimed in ecstacy. "It's dear old honest Ali Baba! Yes, yes, I know! One Christmas time, when yonder solitary child was left here all alone, he *did* come, for the first time, just like that. Poor boy! And Valentine," said Scrooge, "and his wild brother, Orson; there they go! And what's his name, who was put down in his drawers, asleep, at the Gate of Damascus; don't you see him! And the Sultan's Groom turned upside-down by the Genii; there he is upon his head! Serve him right. I'm glad of it. What business had *he* to be married to the Princess!"

Scrooge's emphasis on the unfairness of the marriage of the Sultan's Groom to the Princess probably helps to explain his grudge against his father. We may suppose that Scrooge's father not only separated him from his beloved sister but also treated his

mother badly: "What business had *he* to be married to [her]."
This hypothesis is supported by Little Fan's remark when she
came to take Scrooge home: "Father is so much kinder than he
used to be. . . ."

Please note the change that begins to take place in Scrooge
when he is reminded by the Ghost of Christmas Past of his old
transitional objects. With "[h]is heart and soul . . . in the scene,
and with his former self" he thinks it "strange" that he could
ever have forgotten those special relationships. This is mindful of
a clinical observation that I have made many times: Patients,
when asked about their childhood transitional objects, usually
break into a smile—regardless of how depressed or disturbed they
may be—and describe their old soothers with a genuineness and
openness that may be quite out of character for them. Dickens describes further the effects of Scrooge's contemplation of his old
transitional objects, his favorite stories: "To hear Scrooge ex-
pending all the earnestness of his nature on such subjects, in a
most extraordinary voice between laughing and crying; and to see
his heightened and excited face; would have been a surprise to his
business friends in the city, indeed." Continuing:

> "There's the Parrot!" cried Scrooge. "Green body and
> yellow tail, with a thing like a lettuce growing out of the top of
> his head; there he is! Poor Robin Crusoe, he called him, when
> he came home again after sailing around the island. Poor
> Robin Crusoe, where have you been Robin Crusoe? The man
> thought he was dreaming, but he wasn't. It was the Parrot,
> you know. There goes Friday, running for his life to the little
> creek! Halloa! Hoop! Halloa!"
> Then, with a rapidity of transition very foreign to his usual
> character, he said, in pity for his former self, "Poor boy" and
> cried again.

The lonely boy turned to books for soothing. Suddenly, Ali
Baba came to comfort him. Like David Copperfield, the youthful
Scrooge could find soothing through psychological union with
things external to himself. However, by the time he is a young
man he has come to "fear the world too much" and his master-
passion, "gain," has eclipsed his nobler aspirations. His lady

friend tells him that his emotional wounds have not healed and that he is trying to rise above the world's reproaches through greedy control of all contingencies. Of course, such an aspiration is inimical to the transitional mode because it impairs the ego's autonomy and closes one off to progressive self-object merger.

The Ghost of Christmas Present, like the Ghost of Christmas Past, also helps Scrooge to recover his ability for transitional experience:

> Scrooge's niece played well upon the harp; and played among other tunes a simple little air . . . which had been familiar to the child who fetched Scrooge from the boardingschool, as he had been reminded by the Ghost of Christmas Past. *When this strain of music sounded, all the things that Ghost had shown him, came upon his mind; he softened more and more; and thought that if he could have listened to it often, years ago, he might have cultivated the kindnesses of life* for his own happiness with his own hands, without resorting to the sexton's spade that buried Jacob Marley. [Italics added].*

Thus, *A Christmas Carol* goes beyond David Copperfield in its presentation of transitional relatedness by illustrating factors that may interfere with its development. *A Christmas Carol* also shows something of the possibilities for recovery of the ability for experience in this mode.

The defective ego ideal

In some cases the main problem lies with the failure to establish adequate ego ideals. The ego ideal, like any other psychical acquisition, may be mobilized in the service of the transitional mode. For example, the aspiration to be an artist or composer is perfectly congruent with and nurturant to the transitional mode, that is, to creatively soothing self-object merger. But when, on the other hand, the ego ideals are defective, the cultivation of the transitional mode is impaired or blocked.

*See also McDonald's (1970) explication of the tune as a transitional phenomenon.

O'Neill's short play, *The Dreamy Kid,* may be taken as a concise and moving example of the interference with the capacity for transitional experience by the inculcation of antisocial values. The action concerns a fugitive's return home to see his beloved but dying "Mammy." When he arrives his mouth is "cruel and perpetually drawn back at the corners into a snarl." His dying, ninety-year-old "Mammy" knows nothing of his present difficulties or the change in character that has transpired with his becoming "de boss er de gang." Moreover, his attitude toward her is unaltered: When she asks why he hasn't visited her lately, he answers: "I ain't had de time, Mammy; but you knows I was always game ter give you anything I got. . . . You knows dat, don' you, Mammy?" His "ole Mammy" assumes he is still "de mos' innercent young lamb in de worl'." She asks him if he knows how he acquired his name, Dreamy. Distractedly, he listens to her answer as the lawmen close in:

> MAMMY: [rambling . . . very feebly] Does yo' know—I gives yo' dat name—w'en yo's des a baby—layin' in my arms—
> DREAMY: Yes, Mammy.
> MAMMY: Down by de crik—under de ole willow—whar I uster take yo'—wid yo' big eyes a-chasin'—de sun flitterin' froo de grass—an' out on de water—
> DREAMY: [takes the revolver from his pocket and puts it on top of the chest of drawers] Dey don't get de Dreamy alive— not for de chair! Lawd Jesus, no suh!
> MAMMY: An' yo' was always—a-lookin'—an' a-thinkin' ter yo'se'f—an' yo' big eyes jest a-dreamin' an' a-dreamin'—an' dot's w'en I gives yo' dat nickname— Dreamy—Dreamy—

In the space of just a few pages, O'Neill shows us, with consummate skill, how a sensitive boy, a visionary, who has a deeply loving relationship with his "Mammy"—a relationship based on and supportive of intense self-object merger including even the ability for prayer ("I'm dyin', chile. Hit's de en? You pray for me—out loud—so's I can hear. Oh, Lawd!")—eventually loses his ability for transitional relatedness. Yet the capacity remains

and is rekindled when he learns of his Mammy's failing health
even to the point of going to see her "at de risk o' [his] life."

Objects of the mature transitional mode

Transitional activities early in life—that is, until the end of youth
at around age thirty-four—are soothing principally because of
their evocation of the soothing maternal primary process presence. During the second half of life the underlying oceanic elements become more significant. The maternal link is not lost,
however, as the elderly dying man's cry for his mother may at-
test.

Originally, I had entitled this book, "Beyond the Teddy Bear to
the Oceanic Experience." A mystic friend of mine eagerly read
the manuscript and told me of his disappointment. He asked,
"Where is the part about the oceanic experience?" I explained
that I had sketched it with quotes from several writers and patients and had told something of its psychodynamic nature. He
said, "'Sketched it' is right" and added that it was a "red her-
ring" for me to mention the oceanic experience in the title. He
pointed out that I was, in the main, writing about means rather
than ends; vehicles for solace may or may not lead to oceanic
experiences; there was, according to him, far too little about the
oceanic experience in my book to justify emphasizing it.

My friend has a much better grasp of the ultimate destination of
the whole potential sequence of vehicles for solace than I do. For
example, he states that *within* what the novice calls the oceanic
experience there is a graduated series of object relations analogous to the more concrete and worldly progression from the blanket to the tune, imaginary companion, pet, prayer, spouse, work
of art, etc.; the fledgling mystic typically reacts a bit "hysteri-
cally" to the first dawning of the inner light; the student must then
develop his or her "inward consciousness." I sense, in flashes,
that he is right. However, I am not clear enough about it to be
lucidly expressive and have accepted his advice to concentrate in
this book on the more conventional and tangible vehicles for solace. The closest I will come to describing end-state phenomena is

in the following presentation of a highly refined expression of transitional relatedness. Actually, what I shall say should be taken as mostly in the nature of pointing the reader in the direction of self-discovery. First, let us do a little reviewing.

It is fairly easy for the infant to find suitable transitional objects. The blanket—one of the most frequently chosen early soothers—is structurally simple and appropriate to the infant's relatively undifferentiated means of expression. The aspects of the soothing maternal primary process presence that are first realized in transitional relatedness are usually the warm, the soft, and the tangible. These relationships are sufficiently ubiquitous so that 69.4 percent of the respondents answered "yes" to the following question asked by the *Detroit Free Press:* "A Connecticut psychiatrist says that teddy bears, security blankets and the like are key objects in helping us make a healthy transition from childhood to adulthood, because they help children develop relationships with others. Do you agree?" Typical of the comments were: "My kids made it just fine with blankets and teddy bears"; "If I hadn't had my doll to talk to, I wouldn't have had anyone"; "My little one has the best conversations with his stuffed animals you'd ever want to hear."

The transitional experiencing child's choice of an object may be likened to the dreamer's use of dream images, that is, to the employment of "cheap material . . . ready at hand" (Freud 1900). Diapers, pieces of fuzz, other soft objects, and inert soothers are examples of this "cheap material."

Of course, once the choice is made the material is no longer "cheap," as any parent who tries to eliminate or replace a treasured soother soon learns. The object becomes more expensive with each alteration that its owner makes in it. Therefore, mothers may not be permitted to wash the filthy blanket. They are embarrassed when the soiled old diaper must go along to the store, to church, or to the front door to greet the visitor. Similarly, parents of pre-teenaged children may be puzzled and annoyed at the latter's enthusiastic collecting of beer cans and bottle caps. One very bright eleven-year-old boy disconcerted his parents by darting into Manhattan gutters to retrieve "excellent" beer bottle caps regardless of the fact that he was well-dressed and otherwise behaviorally decorous. Parents of his peers reported that their children showed similar bottle-cap behavior.

It is usually not worth it to the parents—let alone advisable—to oppose these transitional activities. The younger child, in particular, can be a formidable opponent if the mother tries to take away the treasured soother. These objects are often most obtrusive just when the child is wrestling with crucial issues of autonomy.

In any case, it all passes. The objects that the parents may find so repellent are eventually and spontaneously given up as a result of continuing ego development. (Many parents actually become sentimentally attached to the old, ragged stuffed animal that is relegated to the back of the closet.) Maturation is accompanied by increasing sensitiveness to the qualities of potential solacing objects. The blanket and bottle cap cease doing the trick. Emerson referred to this process as growing "expensive and sophisticated" (1954, p. 13). For him, Nature replaced many lesser solacing objects.

Normally, the blanket or piece of fuzz are merely among the earliest objects in a lifelong sequence of relationships to increasingly complex and abstract solacers. Any object may suffice as long as it lends itself to interpretation as a representative of the soothing maternal primary process presence. Typical intermediate objects are imaginary companions, trinkets, tunes, fairy tales, poetry, super and folk heroes, religious figures, prayers, works of art, the fair maiden or handsome prince, mentors, the church, spouses, lovers, friends, and the cabin at Innisfree. Relationships with these objects serve not only to protect us from, in Matthew Arnold's words, "confused alarms of struggle and flight" on a "darkling plain" but, equally important, to orient us to the next stage in finding the highest good in ourselves and others.

This developmental process may achieve considerable refinement and lead to the awareness of unconventional objects. As an example of a penultimate solacing state, let us consider the use of Mozart's opera, *The Magic Flute,* by the Swedish genius, Ingmar

Bergman. In his film of *The Magic Flute,* Bergman presented
Mozart's opera from a behind-the-scenes perspective. Thus, the
filmgoer—that is, us—is first shown the actual opera house, the
audience waiting for the opera to begin, and the musicians
warming up. Mozart's stirring summons to attention is accompanied by a majestic and keynote salute to ancient Greek
statuary. One interviewer has suggested that Bergman believes in
the idea of the artist as a man sent by God, and who *suffers* from a
Platonic belief in inspiration. In support of this is Bergman's
comment: "I can never get shot of them, the fanatics. Whether
they appear as religious fanatics or vegetarian fanatics makes no
odds. They're catastrophic people. These types whose whole cast
of mind as it were looks beyond mere human beings toward some
unknown goal" (Bergman 1973, p. 117).

The camera pans the audience and selects a charming child. It
focuses on her, lingers, and then, in cadence with the overture,
scrutinizes other faces in the audience, periodically returning to
the contemplative young girl. Intervening faces are bracingly and
strikingly heterogeneous. Each visit draws us closer to the individual emotional ambience. The girl's pleasing features become
less interesting than the nuance of emotion shown through her
eyes, her age is uncertain and irrelevant; a man's acneiform scars
retreat as the camera reveals an intelligent glint; an elderly woman's wizened face is softened and rejuvenated. As the synthesis of
camera and orchestra begins to work its Bergmanesque spell, all
adventitious distinctions blur, and we lose sight of features, eye
color, dress, nationality, age, walk of life, conventional and
stereotypical notions of appearance. These considerations are
replaced—if the viewer is so disposed—first by expectant excitement and then—with inner silence—by a joyful affirmation of
some difficult to define but utterly essential deeper unity with
qualities both a part of and beyond the human condition.

The Magic Flute provided the spiritual inspiration for an earlier
but poorly understood Bergman film, *The Hour of the Wolf.* A
group of people meet at a remote castle for dinner. The atmosphere is cold, terrifying, and demonic. Monstrous powers engulf
the participants and a "materialized destructiveness" weighs

them down. They attack and humiliate each other and themselves. The conversation over dinner is brutal and sadistic. When dinner is finished the host presents a toy-theater recital from *The Magic Flute*. The guests gather around, still disoriented by the preceding emotional violence. The tiny figure of Tamino comes into view at center stage. As he sings in profound despair it becomes clear that the "puppet" is actually a real man in miniature. Tamino begins his declaration to the old Priest. Thoughtfully, a man in the audience removes his glasses. Others become transfixed as if by an inner light. Tamino pleads: "Oh, unending night, when will you end?" At the precise moment when the hidden chorus answers him, the faces in the audience are transfigured. The creases of fear, rage, defeat, shame, frustration, and slackness vanish. Something long forgotten is recognized, and there is a moment of transcendent unity among those on the lonely island—a solacing epiphanic respite.

Bergman's Platonically oriented interpretation of *The Magic Flute* is, in addition to a tribute to Mozart, a cinematic representation of the substance of illusion. It blends the sublimity of Mozart's music with the Platonic ideas of the proper order of going from the concrete and worldly to the abstract and heavenly.

Socrates was one of the first to offer an overview of the sequence of object relationships that must be pursued in search of the good life. This extraordinary man, who possessed an "internal sign" (the *Republic*), who "[had] a way of stopping anywhere and losing himself without any reason" *(Symposium)* and who was blessed with "heaven-sent madness" *(Phaedrus)*, also prescribed the means. He identified a transitional mode and said that it was this that made up the rungs of the ladder of progressive object relationships. He called the transitional mode "Love." Love was a great spirit, an "intermediate" between the divine and the mortal, an interpreter or mediator that permitted God and man to "mingle." Love was to be admired, not for its nature, but for its special function of bridging the gap between the mortal and the immortal. Thus, Socrates described a "due order and succession" in the contemplation of objects, with "Love" the invariant means and "birth in beauty" the ultimate goal.

As might be expected on the basis of the connection between transitional relatedness and the maternal primary process presence, Socrates himself was instructed in these mysteries by a *woman*, the wise Diotima of Mantineia.

Perhaps it is not particularly germane to discuss the Platonic theory of forms—a theory espoused by Socrates in the *Republic*, the *Symposium*, the *Phaedo*, and elsewhere, and revived by Ingmar Bergman. For one thing it borders on—indeed, crosses into—end-state territory. Psychiatrists rarely deal with these issues clinically, nor are psychiatrists and physician psychoanalysts usually much interested in such esoteric matters. Even if I could write cogently about higher-order transitional object relations, there probably would not be much of a readership. The cinematic presentation of the due order and succession of the exceptional adult's solacing object relationships is certain to have greater interest value than a review by me of those presumably outmoded and unscientific essays that some of us read as adolescents. Bergman's genius notwithstanding, I heard a psychiatrist friend state that the film of *The Magic Flute* left him cold and wondering why Mozart would write such a silly opera.

The Ecclesiastic existentialism and positivism that dominate the mental health profession make it difficult to find a forum to discuss many aspects of ordinary human relatedness, let alone discuss solacing other-worldly relationships. The division of object relations into dyadic (symbiotic) and triadic (oedipal) kinds is presumed adequate to explain creativity, morality, love, sexuality, group living, and religious experience. (Greenacre's [1957] concept of "collective alternates" is merely a refinement of this essentially positivistic orientation.)

Authors of interdisciplinary repute (see, e.g., Jung 1933, p. 240; 1965, pp. 149–50; Ellison 1979; Küng 1979, p. 11) have expressed the need for mental health professionals to graduate to a theory that admits of a larger range of human relationships. Even some classical psychoanalysts are beginning to reconsider their intellectual commitments: Kohut (1977) has written that Freud's intolerance of experiences that he could not wholly understand, control, and master reflected a serious narcissistic injury. Such a perspective, uttered by so great an authority, may make it easier for teachers at our medical schools to begin to express their own latent interest in other modes of relatedness.

For the present, the main reason to contemplate these highly refined transitional manifestations is that they constitute an important counterpoint to violence, death, and destructiveness. This will be explored further in the next chapter, under the heading, "The Central Moral Problem."

5 Transitional Relatedness and Morality

Descriptively, morals may be defined as the "ways people act, or the ways they feel they should act, and the standards they pursue that to a greater or lesser degree actually guide their lives" (Kaplan 1973, p. 32). In this chapter we shall take into account psychodynamic factors and add that moral action is that action taken with awareness of the possibility of personal loss and guided by a transitionally experienced ideal. To say that the ideal is "experienced transitionally" is to say that the driving force of morality is the soothing maternal primary process presence. While acknowledging that cognitive, identificatory, superego, and other factors contribute in varying degrees to the final shape of moral behavior, the soothing maternal primary process is accorded the central role.

Before parsing the above definition, it might be useful to take a brief overview of the two current major moral explanatory systems.

Current moral explanatory systems

Piagetian morality

Piaget has emphasized *cognitive* development in the genesis of normal morality. He has shown that intellectual growth and morality go hand in hand and are inseparable (1932, p. 186). Social "cooperation," a late stage in Piaget's moral schema, is activated by intelligence (1932, p. 172). In order to understand this, we must view the developing child as Piaget sees him.

The small child is dominated by two forces. Initially, he is able to apprehend only his own inner experience. The infant uses the world for its own satisfaction (p. 165). External reality is distorted according to the child's wishes and fantasies. The external, objective world is "assimilated" to the child's needs. The infant is amoral or completely "egocentric." This corresponds to the "sensorimotor" period of cognitive development.

By three or four years of age, the average child is showing signs of budding moral behavior (i.e., he is becoming aware of rules). He knows, for example, that games have rules by which people abide. His primitive intelligence does not yet, however, permit him to do more than play at rules:

> A three-year-old boy asked his father to play "Battleship" with him. He had seen his older brother playing the game and evidently wished to imitate him. Appropriately enough, he offered his father one section of the game and kept one for himself. The father, who had never played the game, opened it and discovered that one axis of a grid was lined with the alphabet, the other with numbers. To play the game correctly required the plotting of coordinates—an intellectual task far beyond the three-year-old level. He tried to explain to his son that he must first learn the alphabet and how to count in order to play. Undismayed, the boy proceeded by handing him white pegs, red pegs, taking some himself and exchanging various ships. He became slightly impatient when his father did not automatically start to plug pegs into the grids. At first the father was a little confused, since his son's version of the game did not have consistent or understandable rules. Yet it appeared that the boy was observing some rules, or at least his idea of rules, and that he expected his father to abide by his ritual. After they played in this manner for ten minutes or so, the boy suddenly slammed shut his box of pegs and ships and, standing up, announced, "Ok, I win, you lose!"

This boy was showing signs of nascent Piagetian morality. He was vaguely aware of the fact that rules were supposed to govern both of their behaviors. Yet he "assimilated" both the rules and his father to his own egocentric view of the world.

At five or six years of age the normal child is well on the way to developing a new morality. Rules are in much sharper focus for him, and he can play "Battleship" as it is intended. He expects that all who play will abide by the same rules. Yet the five-year-old's rules typically retain an egocentric ("preoperational") quality, and cognitive limitations are grossly apparent. The normal five-year-old believes that the coin thrown from one hand to the other has magically migrated to his ear and that an amount of liquid poured into a tall thin glass is greater than the same amount poured before his eyes into a short fat glass. Interest in cartoons and science fiction is high, and Yogi Bear is as alive as any other creature. This magic-laden, scotomatous cognition makes rules sacrosanct. There is a correlative belief in the supernatural as exemplified by attachment to superheroes. The five-year-old believes that he can actually become the Six-Million-Dollar Man, the Incredible Hulk, or Batman. Belief in supernatural powers—whether internalized or projected—colors the child's morality and fertilizes the soil for implantation of specific religious, cultural, and familiar beliefs such as in Jesus, Santa Claus, leprechauns, the Easter Bunny, and the mythically proportioned ancestor.

By the age of ten to twelve years another moral stage is reached. The animism and magical thinking recede in importance. The ten-year-old sees that adherence to rules is often negotiable among peers. At least some of the rules are not sacrosanct. Thus, children on the playground may argue over an interpretation of a baseball rule, campaign for a particular view, threaten, cajole, appeal to each other's common sense and good intentions, and even agree to vote on exactly how the game should be played. Children at this age begin seriously to "accommodate" to differing and opposing views.

There is much debate about the timing and sequence of these moral-cognitive developments, and some observers question the universality of the phenomena described by Piaget (Favazza and Oman 1978). However, there is consensus regarding two Piagetian conclusions: that moral development from infancy to old age normally entails a progressive decentering, a shift in cognitive emphasis from awareness of only one perspective; and that maturation is accompanied by a demystification of the rules by which we live. The magical and supernatural give way to the matter-of-fact and negotiable.

The origin of morality in Piaget's theory is a "spontaneous mutual affection" (p. 195) between mother and child which "from the first prompts the child to acts of generosity, and even of self-sacrifice, to very touching demonstrations which are in no way prescribed. And here no doubt is the starting point for that morality of good which we shall see developing alongside of the morality of right or duty and which in some persons completely replaces it" (p. 195). Searching for the wellspring of morality, he says: "Nothing is more characteristic of childhood memories than this complex sensation of gaining access to one's most intimate possessions and at the same time of being dominated by something greater than oneself which seems like a source of inspiration. . . . It may be that the genesis of these experiences is to be sought in the unique situation of the very young child in relation to adults. The theory of the filial origin of the religious sense seems to us singularly convincing in this connection" (p. 94). Elsewhere Piaget refers to the primary condition of moral life as the "need for reciprocal affection" (p. 176).

With respect to what keeps moral behavior unfolding, Piaget observes that

> everything conspires to impress upon the baby the notion of regularity. Certain physical events (alternation of day and night, sameness of scenery during walks, etc.) are repeated with sufficient accuracy to produce an awareness of "law," or at any rate to favor the appearance of motor schemes of prevision. The parents, moreover, impose upon the baby a certain number of moral obligations, the source of further regularities (meals, bed-time, cleanliness, etc.) which are completely (and to the child indissociably) connected with the external regularities. From its earliest months the child is therefore bathed in an atmosphere of rules . . . [P. 52]

He adds to this impress of infantile regularity the factor of group living: "The mere fact of individuals living in groups is sufficient to give rise to new features of obligation and regularity in their lives. The pressure of the group upon the individual would thus explain the appearance of this sui generis feeling which we call respect and which is the source of all religion and morality" (p. 101).

Of course, a great deal more could be said about Piaget's moral scheme. This is not intended to be a complete exposition but is offered for the purpose of orientation to the discussion to follow.

Let us consider the second major explanatory framework.

Freudian morality

Classical psychoanalytic moral theory is complementary to Piaget's cognitive moral theory because it emphasizes the role of the unconscious, emotional, and irrational in the formulation of moral laws and rules. Freud's description of unconscious motivation and conflict, and his formulations of the superego and ego ideal, have been among the most important contributions by a psychiatrist to the foundation of a moral science.

In addition, Freudian psychoanalysis has addressed the causes of some instances of immoral behavior. Criminality resulting from a sense of guilt is an example of a clinically useful psychoanalytic paradigm.

Freud claimed that the oedipus complex was the origin of morality and the forerunner of the psychological structure, the superego. Moral behavior was regarded as the by-product of conflict between the inmost essence of human nature: the elemental instincts, on the one hand, and the parental and societal standards and prohibitions, on the other. Good and noble beginnings were seen as adjuncts in the genesis of morality.

Freud's psychology of morality constituted a methodological departure from previous ethical systems because it was based mainly on fairly systematic clinical observations of how people grow, change, and behave. His was perhaps the first theory to ground values in human nature as defined by scientific study of patients.

The superego is presumed to be the last of the psychic organizations to devleop. Parental prohibitions and attitudes, including loving attitudes, toward the self are internalized and are reflected partly in the conscious sector of the superego, the "conscience" or the "imperativistic" (Hartmann 1960, p. 280) agency.

The goal-seeking facet of the superego is the "ego ideal." (This is the part of the superego that must be distinguished clinically and metapsychologically from the transitional mode and the psychological structures that subserve it; see chap. 2.) Laufer's definition (1964, p. 200) will suffice for this overview: "[The] *ego ideal* [is] that part of the superego which contains images and attributes the ego strives to acquire in order to re-establish narcissistic equilibrium." Blos (1974), in apparent agreement with Laufer, points out that the roots of the ego ideal "lie in primary narcissism. It perpetuates, so to say, an eternal approximation to the narcissistic perfection of infancy" (p. 51).

There are differing opinions about when the ego ideal is finally established. Ritvo (1971, p. 255) sees the ego ideal as becoming a "structuralized institution" of the mind only toward the end of adolescence, whereas Laufer (1964, p. 201) believes that the ego ideal (and the superego as a whole) is well established by the time of latency. Blos (1974), echoing Freud, reminds us that the ego ideal is the "heir of the negative oedipus complex" (p. 46).

Exactly when the ego ideal and conscience are finally established is not as important for the present purpose as when and how they originate. According to Freud (1932), the oedipus complex "makes way" for the superego, and the latter is established only when the former is dissolved or "smashed to pieces" (p. 92). However, Loewald (1962) reminds us that the *origins* of the superego are to be found not only in the period of dissolution of the oedipus complex but also in the period of direct or immediate identifications occurring before the oedipal phase proper. "Thus we can distinguish two types or stages of identification: those that precede, and are the basis for object cathexis, and those that are the outcome of object cathexes formed in the oedipal phase." Although Loewald believes that "Freud underplayed, when it comes to early psychic stages, the crucial importance of the individual psychic environment" (Loewald 1972, p. 243) there is evidence that he was at least aware of it: "At first, the human organism is incapable of bringing about the specific action. It takes place by *extraneous help*, when the attention of an experienced person is drawn to the child's state by discharge along the path of internal change. In this way this path of discharge acquires a secondary function of the highest importance, that of *communication*, and the initial helplessness of human beings is the *primal source* of all *moral motives*" (Freud 1895). It is regrettable that Freud did not explain this delphic statement about the "primal source" of morality. His later moral theory largely contradicted this insight.

Piaget and Freud: What is not explained

Better than anyone else, Piaget has helped us to understand the role of cognitive factors in the internalization of specific moral rules. In a very general way, he has also made a contribution to understanding the ultimate source of morality.

He explicitly connects moral development with the influence of the mother. However, he does not tell us very much about the nature of this "spontaneous mutual affection," this "something greater than oneself," this essential "need for reciprocal affection."

Nor does Piaget explain how it is that a clinically significant number of people grow up completely refractory to rules in the moral domain. Psychopaths reason as well as or better than normals about moral situations (Link, Scherer, and Byrne 1978). One has only to listen to a number of psychopaths talk about how they "outsmarted" normals—"beat them at their own game"—to realize that the moral problem of the psychopath is not cognitive. Steinbeck (1970) has the quintessential psychopath describe her perspective about normal morality. When asked why she "hate[s]

so much" she replies: "It isn't hatred, it's contempt. When I was
a little girl I knew what stupid lying fools they were—my own
mother and father pretending goodness. And they weren't good. I
knew them. I could make them do whatever I wanted. I could
always make people do what I wanted. When I was half-grown I
made a man kill himself. He pretended to be good too..." (p.
370).

It does not help the clinician much to suggest that the
psychopath lacks the "sui generis" feeling, or that he is unresponsive to the "mere fact of individuals living in groups," or
that he lacks the capacity for "spontaneous mutual affection" (p.
195). Such statements are similar to saying that language is "ge-
netically determined." It is cul-de-sac theorizing. A fully satisfactory and clinically applicable moral theory must take into account the all too many instances of virtually aborted moral development.

Classical psychoanalytic theory has gone beyond Piagetian
theory in explaining certain moral aberrations. However, Freudian psychoanalysis has not, in reality, shed much light on the
origin of morality. This is partly because classical psychoanalysts
have not scrutinized potential early pre-oedipal roots; psychoanalysis is not a good investigative technique for preverbal states.
Moreover, insofar as psychoanalytic theorists have applied their
technique to analyzable patients, they have worked with a very
restricted part of the clinical spectrum. To identify the source of
morality we must examine those patients in whom it is largely if
not completely lacking. Such patients do not ask for psychoanalytic treatment:

> There seems to be considerable variability in the degree of
> polymorphous perverse development in psychopathic charac-
> ters and in criminals. These people, of whatever type, do not
> often come to the analyst and one must search biographies,
> novels as well as scientific literature and the annals of crime to
> get reports. . . . This is a difficult field for the analyst for it is
> one in which there really is no chance to analyze the patients.
> The only contributions that psychoanalysis can make are

based on deductions derived from the psychoanalytic treatment of less severe cases and on the study of the rare biographical accounts of individual criminals. [Greenacre 1968]

A salient nonpsychoanalytic clinical example of a psychopathic character may be taken from our study (Horton et al. 1974) of the relationship between personality disorder and transitional relatedness:

An eighteen-year-old marine who had destroyed a barracks "for the fun of it," assaulted an officer, deserted his post, and required repeated, unsuccessful disciplinary action, described, as part of his childhood, enuresis, arson, and delight in "hanging cats." He recollected only one toy (and no soothers) from early childhood and said: "I got a steam shovel for Christmas when I was about six. My mother gave it to me. You know what the first thing I did with it was? I beat the fuck out of it! I didn't play with things. All I liked to do was go out in the woods and cut down trees, or hunt and fish."

This case is cited to help reinforce the awareness of how deeply rooted moral disturbances can be. The patient was highly intelligent, knew the rules, and yet chose to ignore them. Such amorality is not satisfactorily explained by either classical psychoanalytic theory or Kohut's new psychology of the self. Neither psychology addresses the problem of the truly selfless person, the "subtly constructed reflex machine" described by Cleckley (1941, p. 259) and others.

Overlooked by the superego theorists are several other crucial facts. For example, a relationship with a father—triadic conflict—is not necessary for the development of morality. Although the Copperfield example is not, strictly speaking, a case study, it illustrates the inessential role of the father in the genesis of morality. Copperfield's father was dead before David's birth. The sadistic Murdstone, David's stepfather, did not appear until David was in latency and could not possibly have been the nidus for Copperfield's moral development. Case study or not, it is a fact that posthumous children are often as moral as anybody else. There is also the observation that people who either have not resolved triadic conflicts or have regressed from them may have values, standards, and codes that they faithfully pursue. This is because the capacity for ego-syntonic merger with objects external to the self—whether another person, inanimate object, cultural institution, rule of conduct, or moral law—is established prior to and independently of oedipal conflict resolution.

The central moral problem

A satisfactory moral theory must offer an account of why people may wish to kill. To kill and particularly to take pleasure in killing is the ultimate moral problem of this or any age. Just this week a national newsmagazine carried a story, pictures included, on Brazilian "death squads"—vigilante groups that not only murder their victims but also inflict burns, savage beatings, and castration in the process. Another story in the same edition contained a photograph of a Liberian execution team celebrating over the just-killed bodies of political prisoners. A few feet away from the assembled executioners and the hunched-over corpses a man and a woman hold hands. The woman smiles broadly at her companion.

Almost any day we can read or hear about awesome human destructiveness directed toward other people, whether in a prison in New Mexico or the Middle East or closer to home. Indeed, a person in the United States is more likely to be killed at home by a family member than anywhere else or by anyone else. Approximately one in four murder victims, not only in the United States but in many other countries as well, is a family member (Gelles and Straus 1979).

This is not a sociological treatise on the sources of violence. I can speak most knowledgeably from the clinical context:

A thirty-year-old head nurse has frequent fantasies—masturbatory and coital—of torturing either men or women. One of her more sadistic fantasies involves using a scalpel on the chest of her bound and gagged victim. From time to time she has had a fleeting impulse to ask one of her sex partners to let her tie them up. However, the mere thought of having another person helpless in her hands makes her "wet" and fearful of losing control. She states: "Hurting them would not be enough—I'm afraid of what I would do."

A twenty-five-year-old mother of two became acutely anxious shortly after the birth of her first son. As a teenager she had performed numerous sexual acts on male children that she had babysat for. She usually used preverbal children—partly because she did not wish to be caught. A five-year-old boy's complaint to his mother scared her and she stopped the practice. Now she was afraid because the memory of those acts was so exciting that she was not sure that she could control herself with her own son.

The wish to exploit, hurt, even to kill others is a nearly ubiquitous human phenomenon. The fact that many people do not let themselves be aware of these impulses does not controvert their existence. My clinical experience dovetails with that of Stoller (1976), who concluded: "We try to make the outlandish folk function as scapegoats for the rest of us, but anyone—analyst or other—who collects erotic thoughts knows that many citizens, avowedly heterosexual, conspicuously normal (not just the subway frotteurs, erotic vomiters, sheep lovers, coprophiliacs, or dirty phone callers) are also filled with hatred and wishes, if not plans, to harm others . . ." (p. 908).

Closely related to wishing for the death of others is wishing for one's own death. The evidence for the existence of self-destructive wishes is preponderant. Putting aside successful suicide, which speaks for itself, we have also to consider the smokers—even those psychoanalysts who lecture on *Beyond the Pleasure Principle* while smoking one cigarette after another—the drinkers, the overeaters, and the motorcyclists, to mention a few. With respect to the motorcyclists, I am not referring just to the hell-bent-for-leather, suicidally macho types. In Bermuda an Island official told me that there had been 216 tourist accidents on motorbikes in the previous month, resulting in broken limbs, concussions, lacerations, and one death. Undoubtedly some of these "accidents" were unmotivated. On the other hand, there must have been a lot of motivated stupidity behind such gross neglect of obvious danger. A Bermuda taxicab driver shook his head incredulously as a motorbiking tourist careened across the road in front of our car, evidently unable to make up his mind which side of the road he should be on.

Freud (1920) postulated the existence of a death instinct to explain murder, suicide, sadomasochism, and the need to repeat self-destructive experiences. Most psychoanalysts reject the death-instinct idea. For example, May (1972), calling the death-instinct theory "strange" (p. 155), suggests an alternative inter-pretation: "When a person has not been loved or has been loved inconsistently or by a mother or father who was himself radically insecure, there develops in his later aggression a penchant for revenge on the world, a need to destroy the world for others in as much as it was not good for him" (p. 159). Kohut (1977)—perhaps the psychoanalyst of greatest stature to recently reject the death instinct—essentially reiterates May's idea: Destructive rage "is always motivated by an injury to the self" (pp. 116–17). These psychological theorists appear to believe, with Bertrand Russell (1957), that "hatred and fear can, with our present psychological knowledge and our present industrial technique, be eliminated altogether from human life" (p. 45).

In contrast, I doubt that the wish to kill or to die can be elimi-nated from a single human being. Even those who live a long life in good health calling for the highest both in feelings and creative-ness may yearn for death. For example, the brilliant Cosima Wagner (1976) spoke repeatedly in her diaries of her and Richard Wagner's death wish. Though she lived until ninety-two years of age she learned that "a human being fights against death all [her] life" (p. 283). Writing from a predominantly Christian point of view, she spoke of the "harsh" dream of life (p. 31), her correla-tive "deep longing for death" (p. 63), the "sin of existence" (p. 731), the "ecstasy of suicide" (p. 709), and the "blessedness" of death (p. 782). For Cosima, life was a "task" (p. 276) and one woke to death (p. 651) as a "test" (p. 224) of life. Like the ancient Greeks—Socrates, Plato, Aristotle, and others—Cosima Wagner viewed death as a transitional stage leading to life on a higher plane.

Cosima's perspective may find support in the recent literature on near-death experiences. Studies of those who have attempted suicide show that some attempters have had transcendental experiences—reunion with deceased loved ones (Buckman and Greyson 1977), feelings of peace and relief, and cosmic unity (Grof and Halifax 1968).

In any event, it seems very clear to me as I hear it from my patients, examine it in myself, and contemplate what people actually do—to themselves and to others—that the wish to die, whatever it may signify ultimately, is to be counted among the most basic of all wishes. When my patient states that she is afraid to experiment with her sadomasochistic impulses because of the possibility of sliding down a slippery slope, she does so with a shudder that conveys an *instinctual* feel.

This chapter began with a definition of morality that must still remain enigmatic. In preparation for a discussion of the definition, I reviewed briefly the cognitive and superego aspects of morality. While acknowledging that cognitive and superego facets exist and contribute to the final shape of moral behavior, I pointed out their limits. Neither theory offers a satisfactory account of the source of morality. The most serious moral aberrations are left largely unexplained and the deeply rooted nature of ubiquitous death wishes is underplayed.

Freud attempted to explain the impulse to kill by invoking a death instinct. Most psychoanalysts reject it as clinically non-contributory. Moreover, coming from the Ecclesiastical tradition (that is, the life-is-meaningless framework) as it does, the concept of a death wish does not permit an examination of the relationship between life and death and possible intermediate states. In the Freudian theory, death is conceived of as an *objectless* condition. It seems that Freud confused utter aloneness with death—a distinction made perspicuous by Ingmar Bergman in *Wild Strawberries*. In that film the elderly doctor, Isak, learned the ironic lesson that to be aloof from and inimical to other people and their needs is to suffer a living death.

Transitional relatedness and the central moral problem

Let us now consider the unique role of transitional relatedness in the development of morality. I am going to suggest that transitional relatedness brings together or coordinates cognitive and superego factors into a cohesive moral whole. This is accomplished in concert with destructive urges. The phrase "in concert with" is most appropriate because transitional relatedness sometimes serves as a defense against death wishes and at other times acts in the service of them. This way of looking at transitional relatedness is perhaps congruent with Modell's description of the transitional object concept as a watershed with a progressive and regressive side.

The severely personality-disordered individual is of special interest due to his or her inability, if not incapacity, for transitional relatedness:

> An intelligent thirty-five-year-old married, childless auto
> salesman was referred for evaluation of competency to stand
> trial on charges of rape. He had forced himself on a pubescent
> neighbor girl. This incident was one of a great many
> crimes—mostly petty—that he had committed beginning in
> early childhood. Frightened, bitter, and resentful, both gener-
> ally and regarding his arrest and likely incarceration, he ex-
> pressed many rationalizations and disclaimers of personal re-
> sponsibility. He could recall no attachments early in life to
> soothing objects. He believed that his mother, like his wife,
> had never been in touch with his needs. Not only had he not
> been able to merge with objects (such as the blanket or stuffed
> animal) that stood fairly immediately for a healthy mother-
> child symbiosis, he had not developed attachments to any
> subsequent things—prayers, poems, superheroes, mythical
> characters, imaginary companions, Santa Claus, angels, good
> luck charms, tunes, etc.—that could represent, more subtly,
> the existence of a soothing maternal primary process pres-
> ence. He was one of those amoral unfortunates who "moves
> through the world wrapped in his separateness, as though in
> an insulator, touched rarely and never moved by his fellow
> man." [Horton et al. 1974]

The above case is similar in its essentials to that of the psychopathic prostitute, Cathy, described by Steinbeck in *East of Eden*. She let no moral barriers stand in her way, murdering, blackmailing, lying where expedient. As a teenager frustrated by her parents' efforts to discipline her, she ran away: "In the morning she was gone. Her straw traveling basket was gone and the best of her clothing. Her bed was neatly made. The room was impersonal—nothing to indicate that a girl had grown up in it. There were no pictures, no mementoes, none of the normal clutter of growing. Cathy had never played with dolls. The room had no Cathy imprint" (p. 95).

Recognition of the fact that well-defined personality-disordered persons lack specifically the ability for transitional relatedness helps us to understand both that condition and morality in general. We need no longer puzzle with Steinbeck about such "monstrous" persons: "Her life may have been her language, formal, developed and indecipherable" (p. 212).

Since we, the vast majority, are capable, in varying degrees, of holding soothing illusions that promote psychological growth and support a sense of oneness with other people, our culture, and its institutions, we tend to find the psychopathically disturbed individual bewildering. It is instructive to see how even experienced psychotherapists are taken in by such persons. These sensitive professionals blind themselves to the reality of the problem by consoling themselves with the idea that psychopathy is a *human* process. Yet the essential nature of the sociopath's psychopathology is less than human.

As is often the case, the novelist anticipates clinically proven insight. Steinbeck knew that there was something missing in psychopathically disordered people. He understood better than generations of clinicians that these troublesome individuals were not simply people in conflict. During a confrontation between the protagonist and Cathy, the sociopathic prostitute, the latter issues a challenge: "What a sweet dreamer is Mr. Mouse! Give me a sermon, Mr. Mouse." Adam's response is on target: "No, I won't because I seem to know that there's a part of you missing. Some men can't see the color green, but they may never know

they can't. I think you are only part of a human. I can't do
anything about that. But I wonder whether you ever feel that
something invisible is all around you."

The question often inappropriately asked of the personality-
disordered criminal is, What was the *motive* for the brutal or
other socially destructive act? What should be asked is how the
sociopath could do otherwise. The fact that even dogs and chimpanzees have the capacity for transitional relatedness, whereas
severely personality-disordered persons do not, has led me to
hypothesize that many sociopaths lack the neuropsychological
wherewithal for sustained moral action (Horton 1976a, 1976b,
1976c). Appositely, MacLean (1964) has explained that when the
psychiatrist bids the patient to lie on the couch, he is actually
inviting a "loosely leashed reptile" (the brainstem) and a
"loosely bridled horse" (the limbic system) to join him. Without
the ability for soothing self-object merger, there is no reliable
leash or bridle. All too easily these dangerous people are pro-
voked to exhibit the naive cruelty of lower animals.

There is irony in the fact that while, on the one hand,
psychopaths lack specifically the ability for soothing self-object
merger, on the other hand, many parents consciously and aggressively seek to disabuse their children of soothing illusions.
I have seen mothers and fathers virtually trip over each other
to make sure that their three- or four-year-old does not believe
in angels, God, or Santa Claus! This is done in the name of
"intellectuality"—*smart* children have no illusions. Clinically,
this proves to be a harmful attitude, the damaging magnitude of
which depends on whether or not the mother was more satisfactorily empathic during the child's infancy. If she was equally
unempathic during the earliest months, the child is likely to grow
up with significant social distortions, becoming, at worst, a
personality-disordered individual. George Sand's pithy remark
said it well: "If a woman is not disillusioned at thirty she is
brainless, but if she has no illusions at twenty she is *heartless.*"

A stark portrayal of a world without soothing illusion is Bergman's film *The Serpent's Egg.* The time is 1923, the place Ber-
lin, where "ordinary people have largely lost faith in both the

present and the future'' (Bergman 1977, p. 1). A trapeze artist,
Abel Rosenberg, arrives at his boarding house and is greeted
warmly by his landlady. A wedding party is going on in another
room. The room is full of people singing, shouting, laughing.
Rosenberg looks in on this happy, peaceful scene and is deeply
reflective. (This is the one heavenly clear ray of sunshine in the
film: It is the gentle Bergmanesque vision of *Wild Strawberries*
and *Smiles of a Summer Night*.) Arriving upstairs at the room
that he and his brother share he discovers his brother with his
brains splattered on the wall—a suicide.

The suicide scene would have been shocking enough whatever
had preceded it. But we are given a double jolt. There was something ultimately *right* about the wedding party: love, family, romance, joy, marriage, play, kindness to the stranger. The remainder of the film is reality at close quarters—an illusionless and
degrading reality. Ordinary starving Germans kill the horse in the
street and eat it where it lies. Those who have no illusions take
advantage of the remaining few who do:

> A thirty-year-old woman with tender feelings for children is
> locked up with a four-month-old baby as part of a ''scientific''
> experiment. She does not know that the infant she has volun-
> teered to care for is brain damaged and will scream con-
> tinuously day and night no matter what she does to relieve it.
> Eventually driven berserk she murders the baby.

Bergman makes it very clear that the failure to develop, nurture,
and sustain soothing illusions or the compulsion to aggressively
destroy them in others is the quintessence of bestiality as only the
human reptile can conceive.

The definition of morality to include a transitionally experienced ideal permits us, therefore, to describe the moral problem
of the most aberrant members of the human community. Yet the
nuclear viciousness shown universally by a small percentage of
any population (see Murphy 1976) is not restricted to them. As I
have tried to suggest, the difference resides in the presence of
other factors that modulate, inhibit, and redirect aggressive
strivings.

The most important psychological counterforce to the death
instinct is the soothing maternal primary process presence and
the constructive transitional mode that originates in this most
essential of all internalizations. The psychopathic patient, who is
devoid of the ability to relate transitionally, often exhibits average
or better cognitive, ego, and superego development. These
people may, for considerable periods of time, show keen awareness of what is expected of them. However, when they do act out
it is with a rage that makes clear their utter isolation from things
external.

Loewald (1972), working with less disturbed patients, has also
encountered "sick" people who are unable to be helped with
conventional psychoanalytic methods: "But in severe cases such
an imbalance is rooted in problems of early psychic development,
in the precursors of morality, conscience, and guilt which ante-
date the oedipus complex and the formation of the superego—
where destructive forces got out of hand, as it were, and affected
the very fiber of the person *before* they could be bound..." (p.
240). Loewald emphasizes the role of the "caring persons" in
stemming the tide of the death instinct. To this it must be added
that the crucial internalization is the soothing maternal primary
process presence that is manifested specifically in transitional
relatedness and the capacity for moral feeling and action. This
internalization is not merely a precursor of morality but rather the
specific cause and major contributor to its expression.

*The relationship of the ego mechanisms of defense and
transitional relatedness in limiting destructiveness*

The ability to relate transitionally is the best single safeguard
against unrestrained destructiveness. However, it is not the only
safeguard. The ego mechanisms of defense play an important
role. Their existence helps to explain why it is that the psychopath is only sporadically destructive. As exemplified in the
introduction, exceptionally aggressive people may function fairly
well most of the time by virtue of the ego mechanisms of defense.
The patient described utilized a variety of defenses ranging in

quality from the narcissistic to the mature. She relied heavily on reaction formations but also and to a lesser extent used altruism, humor, and sublimations.

In fact, the severely personality-disordered person is, except under special conditions, rigidly repressive. Characteristically, he or she does not enjoy sex very much because of brittle reaction formations against pregenital urges. Alcohol is dangerous to these people, and the smarter ones soon learn to avoid even mild intoxication. Fantasy and play are prohibited, as is any kind of experience that may upset the precarious defensive equilibrium.

A thirty-year-old unmarried school administrator brought home to me the necessity of being very careful about attacking a personality-disordered individual's defenses against sexuality. An exceptionally intelligent woman, she had achieved considerable success in her profession despite her nearly total inability to experience soothing psychological union with things or people. Although physically attractive, she had never had intercourse and expressed no desire to other than for the sake of appearances. She literally hated men and their penises. I inferred that the penis symbolized the something terrifyingly missing in her life. She supposed that if she had a penis she too could feel one with the world instead of as a prisoner in a schizoid wasteland. Of course, I did not understand all of this at once. During the first 300 hours of our work together, I misunderstood her: I thought that she suffered with an obsessive-compulsive neurosis and an unusually intense case of penis envy. One incident more than others helped to clarify the nuclear problem. She had complained repeatedly about her height, complexion, features, hair, and foot size. In reality, she was better looking than the average woman. However, it was more important than I had realized that she have available ready-made excuses for continuing her lonely existence. Toward the end of an hour which had begun with her statement that she could never wear shorts because of her ugly legs, I asked, tactlessly: "And how do you feel about showing your genitals?" She became enraged and stated convincingly that she thought seriously of "smashing [me] in the face." After calming down somewhat, she shakily told me a secret: Many years ago she had almost killed someone

by hitting him on the head with a bottle after he had teased her
about her appearance. She said: "I am potentially a very violent person. This is why I don't want people to get close to
me. I don't want them to see what kind of person I really
am."

The above case illustrates two important ideas: (1) the adaptive
ego mechanisms of defense protect against all potentially disruptive instinctual needs, sexual and aggressive; (2) however,
they are better suited for defending against sexual rather than
hostile urges. She, like a great many people, was very successful
in keeping sexual thoughts and feelings out of awareness. In contrast, she had to be continuously on guard against destructive
rage. Her ego mechanisms of defense—projection, passive-
aggressiveness, intellectualization, repression, displacement, reaction formation, and sublimation—were incapable of providing
smooth, reliable protection. When I confronted her with her denial of sexuality, those defenses remained unshaken—it was her
defense-against-aggression house of cards that came tumbling
down.

The reason that transitional relatedness usually provides better
protection than the ego mechanisms of defense against destructive urges is that transitional relatedness is *soothing*. Where the
pleasureless, habitual, and unconscious ego mechanisms of defense serve, in one way or another, to avoid reality, transitional
relatedness is *expressive* of soothing inner reality. The affirmation
of the existence of the soothing maternal primary process presence through the transitional act may actually make the most
frightening, painful, and destructive realities tolerable. Kaplan
(1973) gives a nice example of a wife serving as a transitional
object for her husband in his effort to face death:

> There is a legend of a great sage who had two sons whom he
> loved dearly. On a day when he was away from home, sud-
> denly his two sons died within the same hour. His wife ten-
> derly laid them out in another room and covered them. When
> her husband returned, she said to him, "Many years ago a
> stranger passed this way, and left in my keeping two precious
> jewels. He was gone so long that I felt those jewels were my

own. Today, unexpectedly, he reappeared and demanded that I return to him what is his. Must I, indeed, give them up?'' He said to her, ''How can you doubt where the course of virtue lies?'' She took him by the hand to the other room, threw back the sheet, and said, ''There lie the jewels.''

The sage's wife not only functioned perfectly as a transitional object for her husband but simultaneously supported his adaptive ego mechanisms of defense. We may suppose that she succeeded in soothing her husband with her calmness and preparation and by literally taking his hand. She supported his defenses by giving him—a man who valued understanding—an intellectual point of view about acceptance of untimely death.

Indeed, well-functioning people *blend* transitional and mature defensive activities in coping with destructive internal and external realities. They are able to think openly, flexibly, and constructively about destructive and sexual urges—pregenital as well as genital—in large part because they know that reliable relief from pain through transitional activity is always available.

In striking contrast is a thirty-four-year-old divorced mother of three who was terrified at the thought of losing her physical beauty, and therefore her power over men, as youth drew to a close. She said: ''I've been thinking about what you asked a long time ago regarding toys and special things. My oldest child had a blanket that she carried all over the place when she was a baby. My thirteen-year-old still has her blanket and loads of stuffed pets. My boy has his stuffed animal. But it is true—I've never been able to find relief in anything. Some people can smoke, drink, bite their nails, use drugs, gamble—I haven't even been able to do things like that. It seems that all I have ever been able to do is to see bad things in everybody, including myself.''

The blending of transitional relatedness with primitive or virtually nonexistent mechanisms of defense is not good either. Excessive reliance on transitional soothing in tandem with delusional projection, psychotic denial, distortion, and other narcissistic and immature defenses is found in borderline schizophrenic and schizophrenic conditions and in the borderline syndrome (Arkema 1981; Horton 1977; Modell 1963). In these disorders transitional relatedness is often regressive and may act in the service of the death instinct. The need for unremitting soothing—the inability to tolerate the necessarily painful aspects of reality—leads to the search for a substitute world, even one that may be found only through suicide. These unfortunate people cannot say courageously, with David Copperfield, "I Begin Life on My Own Account, and Don't Like It." Tragically, they all too often take their own lives, and in their angry frustration may take others with them.

*The phrase "moral action is that action taken with
awareness of the possibility of personal loss"*

The phrase "moral action [is] that action taken with awareness of the possibility of personal loss" is included to help distinguish the moral from the trivial, phony, obsessional, or merely ritualistic. True moral action *costs* something; indeed, it connotes sacrifice. Aristotle made explicit this aspect of morality in book 3 of his essay on "Moral Virtue" in *The Nicomachean Ethics*. He said, for example, "It is for facing what is painful . . . that men are called brave" (p. 71). In our time this has been reiterated by the great Lutheran martyr Dietrich Bonhoeffer (1959) in *The Cost of Discipleship*.

This part of the definition also excludes from the category of moral action those deeds performed on the basis of mere stupidity or ignorance of potential personal loss. (Again, Aristotle cogently and persuasively explained the necessity for this stricture in his essay on "Moral Virtue.") To put it somewhat fancifully and symbolically, when the men in the Light Brigade charged, they *knew* that they faced death.

Afterword

A fifty-five-year-old woman with metastatic carcinoma was being hypnotized for pain relief. Asked to recall a happy event from childhood, she related: "I can remember riding on the train as a little girl. My father was going to meet me at the depot. I can still smell the delicious, pungent smoke from the steam engine; and I can see and feel the old velvet curtains, mohair seats, and clean white linen; scrambled eggs and ice cream—the latter served in a silver dish—have never tasted so good; the train swaying gently, the clickety-clack, clickety-clack, the sudden clang, clang, clang and whistle and whoosh of a passing engine—all vividly soothing—live on in my memory." This patient was able to use her childhood memory of the train—intensified by hypnosis—to provide almost complete relief from pain that narcotic analgesics only partially and unsatisfactorily alleviated.

Indeed, vehicles for solace may relieve all sorts of pain, physical as well as mental, emotional, existential, and spiritual. In the above case, the patient and I searched together not only for relief of the agony of metastases but also for escape from the painfully destructive *idea* of an "eroding cancerous condition." This focus provided her with a significant measure of relief.

The single most important idea that I can convey is that understanding transitional phenomena can and should have a crucial role in the assessment and treatment of patients. A young person's means of self-soothing are often prominently visible, or

156

nearly so, and not hard to identify as such. Later in life, the solacing means are likely to be more subtle, even, as Winnicott would have it, "diffused across the whole cultural field." However, mature adults can usually recognize, with a little assistance on the part of the psychiatrist, the sort of thing that is being evaluated and turn it to good use.

Depressed people have often forgotten—at least temporarily —their means of self-soothing. Personality-disordered persons have never developed them and thrash about in their disorientation. The schizophrenically disturbed cling to static objects in a desperate life-saving or life-avoiding effort. Those with the borderline syndrome alternate between the experience of negative, painful affect and only partially successful efforts at using solacing objects.

Identifying a seriously depressed middle-aged person's characteristic avenues of self-soothing and sense of security, and discovering how he or she did it, or tried to do it, just prior to onset of the "endogenous" depression, is frequently as valuable as the prescription of a tricyclic antidepressant. Many hard-to-interpret symptoms become understandable when looked at in terms of vehicles for solace. For example, the "nausea" that some very depressed patients complain of is a result of their dizzying disorientation to solacing objects. One severely depressed young woman was so nauseated during the first several months of her illness that she had the dry heaves every day. When she was finally able to locate a solacing object—in this case, a psychiatrist who reoriented her to her emotional commitments—the nausea remitted and she climbed out of her depression.

More generally, these vehicles for solace are the psychiatrist's—indeed, the physician's—most potent ally in easing the demands of the death instinct. The doctor often plays a pivotal role in their emergence or suppression as constructive forces for change. Particularly important is the recognition that soothing vehicles in the first half of life—until youth ends around age thirty-four—normally facilitate an acceptance of life, whereas vehicles for solace in the second half of life help to make dying a meaningful and even welcome experience. Like tires, leaf springs, and shock absorbers, they render our trip feasible if not comfortable.

I would encourage every psychiatrist to recognize, remember, and relate: recognize the presence—or absence—of transitional phenomena in the patient's personal history and presenting condition, and in how the patient experiences the therapist; remember that transitional phenomena are both hallmarks of and vehicles for development; and relate transitional manifestations to time factors (that is, to the onset of symptoms, to cycle of life, and especially to attitudes toward the future). The ability to sojourn in the intermediate area, to blend feeling and cognition soothingly, to experience psychological union with people and things external and with previously disclaimed parts of the self, is as humanly important as the ability to set ego boundaries, to know the self from the not-self, to be special and separate and in perfect control of one's environment.

The main thesis of this book—that the ability for solacing self-object merger is healthy at every stage in life, and is essential to creative activity of all sorts and to love and morality—may have implications for patterns of child rearing. Should mothers leave their infants in the hands of caretakers for extended periods of time if they can avoid it? If a homeowner asks someone to take care of his or her lawn, plantings, and roses while he is gone, or if a corporation president delegates authority, each may find that the work has not been done with the loving care and precision that he would have given. At least the results of lawn care are fairly immediately visible and the negligence correctable. The effects of a babysitter's influence and the absence of the natural mother are often invisible until it is too late.

The play *Oedipus Rex* was interpreted by Freud to represent a man's guilt over sexual misconduct (i.e., maternal incest and patricide). However, most translations of the myth suggest different predominant motive forces. This is important to what I am saying about the mother's role, because Oedipus Rex appeared to be fairly normal, even exceptional:

True king, giver of laws,
Majestic Oedipus!
No prince in Thebes had ever such renown,
No prince won such grace of power.

This appearance changed when circumstances brought the affectively painful experience of his mother's loss during infancy to the surface. All translations show that Oedipus was abandoned by his mother to be destroyed and that, when he learned or, more precisely, was reminded of this fact, he suffered a rage attack directed against his mother. Calling her an "unspeakable mother" in one translation and a "wretch" in another, he took a sword (in all translations) and went looking for her. Finding her already dead, he enucleated his eyes, not out of guilt, but as a spill-over of rage untamed by a soothing maternal primary process presence. (As far as the motive force of "guilt" goes, Oedipus stated frankly in *Oedipus at Colonus,* "No, I did not sin!")

The development of the ability to accept soothing from another human being, an ability that Oedipus lacked (Jocasta says of him, "Ah, miserable! That is the only word I have for you now. That is the only word I can ever have."), very probably requires the reliable presence of a lovingly nurturant person. Certainly, the studies on transitional relatedness and the interpretation I have given to them in this book lead to this conclusion.

It could be argued that a suitably maternal babysitter might well stimulate the development of the necessary soothing primary process presence. The babysitter might even do a better job than the biological mother. Specifics of maternal and/or caretaker behavior and the timing of such interventions that would insure the development of a soothing presence require elucidation. It is essential that the child be able to develop a sense of a *main* mother. This main mother might, depending on the circumstances, be an aunt, grandmother, or babysitter. Just as the child makes a transitional object, he or she first makes an internal soothing presence to which the transitional object corresponds. For some children this might occur at one or two months of age; for others, there may be a delay of several years. The development of stable transitional relatedness might be a signal that the main mother can begin to let go of her charge. This is because the existence of transitional relatedness shows that the child is already at work on the problem of mastering separation anxiety.

Undoubtedly, the particular combination of child and mother or caretaker and the amount of time given to the relationship are crucial. The ministrations of a loving father are probably better for the production of a soothing structure than those of an aggressive, narcissistic mother. Whether two parents can "share equally"—a current political catchphrase—in helping the child to develop a stable soothing presence is—or should be—open to question. (Political expedience is not a substitute for careful scientific study.) In helping the infant to develop a sense of the main mother, confusion about who that person is should probably be minimized. The Oedipus example speaks to the extreme of this issue: the infant Oedipus was required to give up entirely the initial main mother and to try to create another.

There is, in my experience, some evidence that the "right" parents can juggle parental roles and babysitter to the advantage of the child. However, these have been exceptional parents— mature, sensitive, conscientious, and farsighted. More often I see in my practice the ill effects of the overburdened working mother who, having returned to work during her child's infancy, has committed her child to the care of a relatively unknown and sometimes unsuitable person.

In referring to the "psychotropic influence exerted by social factors," Kohut (1977) describes the recent "shift in man's psychic organization" that is manifested in "disintegration anxiety," a "crumbling self," and inability to experience conflict arising from prolonged emotional intimacy, and an absence of the ability to experience empathic closeness. Perhaps the trend in the decades since World War II for American mothers to rush out of the home into the workplace underlies this regressive shift in adolescent and adult psychopathology.

Lacking certain knowledge in these matters, we must rely on common sense and suppose that it would be good if the overwhelming majority of mothers could once again be supported in feeling that the most noble task a human being can engage in is

that of helping a child to find life essentially agreeable. The offer-
ing of such support is a challenge to the physician in an age when
it is chic to depreciate the role of the mother and homemaker and
to rationalize the emotional abandonment of children.

Of course, the maternal role is only one among many ways of
being creatively nurturant. In a very general way all good
teachers, physicians, friends, and lovers provide this. However, if we measure the importance of a function by its ultimate
impact on the conduct of life—by its delicacy, depth of feeling
and concern, specificity, and generative ramifications—there is
no occupation of greater human significance than that of the caring mother. For it is she, principally, who is instrumental in helping the child to find, and later to offer, vehicles for solace.

References

American Psychoanalytic Association. 1968. *A Glossary of Psychoanalytic Terms and Concepts.* New York: American Psychoanalytic Association.

Aristotle. 1959. *The Nicomachean Ethics of Aristotle.* London: Oxford University Press.

Arkema, P. 1981. The borderline personality and transitional relatedness. *American Journal of Psychiatry* 138 (2):172–77.

Arlow, J. 1963. Conflict, regression, and symptom formation. *International Journal of Psycho-Analysis* 44 (1):12–22.

Arnold, M. 1867. Dover Beach. In C. Brooks and R. Warren, *Understanding Poetry.* New York: Henry Holt & Co., 1952.

Augustine. 1963. *The Confessions of St. Augustine.* Edited by R. Warner. New York: New American Library.

Bak, R. E. 1974. Distortions of the concept of fetishism. *Psychoanalytic Study of the Child* 29:191–213.

Bellow, S. 1976. *To Jerusalem and Back.* New York: Viking Press.

Bergman, I. 1960. *Four Screenplays of Ingmar Bergman.* New York: Simon & Schuster.

———. 1970. *Three Films by Ingmar Bergman.* New York: Grove Press.

———. 1973. *Bergman on Bergman.* New York: Simon & Schuster.

———. 1977. *The Serpent's Egg.* New York: Bantam Press.

Blos, P. 1974. The genealogy of the ego ideal. *Psychoanalytic Study of the Child* 29:43–89.

Bonhoeffer, D. 1959. *The Cost of Discipleship.* New York: Macmillan Co.

Boniface, D., and Graham, P. 1977. The three-year-old and his attachment to a special soft object. *Journal of Child Psychology and Psychiatry.* 20:217–24.

Bowlby, J. 1969. *Attachment and Loss.* Vol. 1, *Attachment.* New York: Basic Books.

Buckman, J., and Greyson, C. B. 1977. Attempted suicide and bereavement: symbiosis, ambivalence, and magical reunion. In B. L. Danta and A. H. Kutscher, eds. *Suicide and Bereavement*. New York: Foundation of Thanatology.

Busch, F. 1977. Theme and variation in the development of the first transitional object. *International Journal of Psycho-Analysis* 58:479–86.

————; Nagera, H.; McKnight, J.; and Pezzarossi, G. 1973. Primary transitional objects. *Journal of the American Academy of Child Psychiatry* 12:193–214.

Chomsky, N. 1978. Speech given to the American Psychoanalytic Association, Winter, New York City.

Cleckley, H. M. 1941. *The Mask of Sanity*. St. Louis: C. V. Mosby Co.

Coppolillo, H. P. 1967. Maturational aspects of the transitional phenomenon. *International Journal of Psycho-Analysis* 48:237–46.

————. 1976. The transitional phenomenon revisited. *Journal of the American Academy of Child Psychiatry* 15(1):36–47.

Davidson, L. 1976. Inanimate objects in psychoanalysis and their relation to transitional objects. *Contemporary Psychoanalysis* 12(4):479–89.

Dickens, C. 1843. *A Christmas Carol*. London: Chapman & Hall.

————. 1950. *David Copperfield*. New York: Random House/Modern Library.

Ehrenberg, D. B. 1976. "The intimate edge" and the "third area." *Contemporary Psychoanalysis* 12(4):489–95.

Ellison, J. 1968. *Life's Second Half—The Pleasures of Aging*. Old Greenwich, Conn.: Devin-Adair Co.

Emerson, R. W. 1850. *Representative Men*. New York: H. M. Caldwell Co.

————. 1954. *Basic Selections from Emerson*. New York: New American Library/Mentor Books.

Escalona, S. K. 1963. Patterns of infantile experience and the developmental process. *Psychoanalytic Study of the Child* 18:197–244.

Favazza, A., and Oman, M. 1978. Foundations of cultural psychiatry: an overview. *American Journal of Psychiatry* 135(3):293–303.

Fenichel, O. 1945. *The Psychoanalytic Theory of Neurosis*. New York: W. W. Norton & Co.

Ferenczi, S. 1913. Stages in the development of the sense of reality. *Sex in Psychoanalysis*. New York: Basic Books, 1950.

Fraiberg, S. 1969. Libidinal object constancy and mental representation. *Psychoanalytic Study of the Child* 24:9–47.

Freud, A. 1963. The concept of developmental lines. *Psychoanalytic Study of the Child* 18:245–65.

Freud, S. 1893. Sketches for the "preliminary communication" of 1893, (B) "III." *Standard Edition* 1:149. London: Hogarth Press, 1950.
———. 1895. Project for a scientific psychology. *Standard Edition* 1:283–397. London: Hogarth Press, 1950.
———. 1899. Screen memories. *Standard Edition* 3:303–22. London: Hogarth Press, 1962.
———. 1900. The interpretation of dreams. *Standard Edition* Vols. 4–5. London: Hogarth Press, 1953.
———. 1909. Analysis of a phobia in a five-year-old-boy. *Standard Edition* 10:3–148. London: Hogarth Press, 1955.
———. 1911. Formulations on the two principles of mental functioning. *Standard Edition* 12:213–26. London: Hogarth Press, 1958.
———. 1914. On narcissism: an introduction. *Standard Edition* 14:67–102. London: Hogarth Press, 1957.
———. 1920. Beyond the pleasure principle. *Standard Edition* 18:7–64. London: Hogarth Press, 1955.
———. 1927. Civilization and its discontents. *Standard Edition* 21:64–145. London: Hogarth Press, 1961.
———. 1932. New introductory lectures on psycho-analysis. *Standard Edition* 22:5–182. London: Hogarth Press, 1964.
Gaddini, R. 1975. The concept of transitional object. *Journal of the American Academy of Child Psychiatry* 14:731–36.
Gaensbauer, T. 1980. Anaclitic depression in a three-and-one-half-month-old child. *American Journal of Psychiatry* 137(7):841–42.
Gallup Poll. 1976. 31% experience religious "union." *Hartford Courant,* December 10.
Gelles, R. J., and Straus, M. A. 1979. Violence in the American family. *Journal of Social Issues,* vol. 35, no. 2.
Greenacre, P. 1957. The childhood of the artist: libidinal phase development and giftedness. *Psychoanalytic Study of the Child* 12:47–72.
———. 1958. The family romance of the artist. *Psychoanalytic Study of the Child* 13:19–36.
———. 1968. Perversions: general considerations regarding their genetic and dynamic background. *Emotional Growth* 1:300–314.
———. 1969. The fetish and the transitional object. *Psychoanalytic Study of the Child* 24:144–64.
Grinker, R.; Werble, B.; and Drye, R. 1968. *The Borderline Syndrome.* New York: Basic Books.
Grof, S., and Halifax, J. 1968. *The Human Encounter with Death.* New York: E. P. Dutton.
Group for the Advancement of Psychiatry. 1976. *Mysticism: Spiritual Quest or Psychic Disorder?* GAP Report, vol. 9, no. 97. New York: Group for the Advancement of Psychiatry.

Harlow, H. F. 1959. Love in infant monkeys. *Scientific American* 200:68–74.

Hartmann, H. 1939. *Ego Psychology and the Problem of Adaptation.* New York: International Universities Press, 1958.

————. 1960. *Psychoanalysis and moral Values.* New York: International Universities Press.

Heiman, M. 1976. Psychoanalytic observations on the last painting and suicide of Vincent Van Gogh. *International Journal of Psycho-Analysis* 57:71–79.

Hemingway, E. 1940. *For Whom the Bell Tolls.* New York: Charles Scribner's Sons.

Hong, M. D. 1978. Transitional phenomena: a theoretical integration. *Psychoanalytic Study of the Child* 33:47–79.

Horton, P. C. 1973. The mystical experience as a suicide preventive. *American Journal of Psychiatry* 130:294–96.

————. 1974. The mystical experience: substance of an illusion. *Journal of the American Psychoanalytic Association* 22:363–80.

————. 1976a. Personality disorder and parietal lobe dysfunction. *American Journal of Psychiatry* 133:782–85.

————. 1976b. The psychological treatment of personality disorder. *American Journal of Psychiatry* 133:262–65.

————. 1976c. Organic brain dysfunction and personality disorder: Dr. Horton replies. *American Journal of Psychiatry* 133:1470–71.

————. 1977. Personality disorder and hard-to-diagnose schizophrenia. *Journal of Operational Psychiatry* 8(2):70–81.

————. 1978. The Restoration of the Self (book review). *Journal of Operational Psychiatry* 9(2):72–74.

————; Louy, J.; and Coppolillo, H. P. 1974. Personality disorder and transitional relatedness. *Archives of General Psychiatry* 30:618–22.

Husserl, E. 1962. *Ideas.* New York: MacMillan.

Jacobson, E. 1964. *The Self and the Object World.* New York: International Universities Press.

James, W. 1902. *The Varieties of Religious Experience.* New York: Random House/Modern Library, 1929.

John of the Cross. 1967. From *The Poems of St. John of the Cross.* Edited by R. Campbell. New York: Grosset & Dunlap.

Johnson, D. 1960. From an essay, quoting Bruno Walter, on record jacket of Wagner's Overture to *Die Meistersinger* etc. Columbia Masterworks, MS6149, Library of Congress Catalog no. R60-1119.

Jung, C. G. 1933. *Modern Man in Search of a Soul.* New York: Harcourt, Brace & World.

————. 1965. *Memories, Dreams, Reflections.* New York: Vintage Books.

Kafka, J. S. 1969. The body as transitional object: a psychoanalytic study of a self-mutilating patient. *British Journal of Medical Psychology* 42:207–12.

Kahne, M. J. 1967. On the persistence of transitional phenomena into adult life. *International Journal of Psycho-Analysis* 48:247–58.

Kaplan, A. 1964. *The Conduct of Inquiry*. San Francisco: Chandler Publishing Co.

———. 1967. A philosophical discussion of normality. *Archives of General Psychiatry* 17:325–30.

———. 1973. *Love . . . and Death*. Ann Arbor: University of Michigan Press.

Kavka, J. 1978. Discussion of "transitional relatedness as a developmental line." Paper presented at the Spring meeting of the American Psychoanalytic Association, Atlanta, Georgia.

Kernberg, O. 1970. A psychoanalytic classification of character pathology. *Journal of the American Psychoanalytic Association* 18(4):743–68.

Kobbé, G. 1972. *Kobbé's Complete Opera Book*. Edited by the Earl of Harewood. New York: G. P. Putnam's Sons.

Kohut, H. 1966. Forms and transformations of narcissism. *Journal of the American Psychoanalytic Association* 14:243–72.

———. 1971. *The Analysis of the Self*. New York: International Universities Press.

———. 1977. *The Restoration of the Self*. New York: International Universities Press.

Kollar, E. 1972. Object relations and the origin of tools. *Archives of General Psychiatry* 26:23–27.

Kris, E. 1952. *Psychoanalytic Explorations in Art*. New York: International Universities Press.

———. 1962. Decline and recovery in the life of a three year old. *Psychoanalytic Study of the Child* 17:175–215.

Küng, H. 1979. *Freud and the Problem of God*. New Haven, Conn.: Yale University Press.

Laufer, M. 1964. Ego ideal and pseudo ego ideal in adolescence. *Psychoanalytic Study of the Child* 19:196–221.

Leavy, S. 1978. Language and psychoanalysis. *Journal of the American Psychoanalytic Association* 26:633–39.

Lidz, T. 1973. *The Origin and Treatment of Schizophrenic Disorders*. New York: Basic Books.

———; Fleck, S.; and Cornelison, A. R. 1966. *Schizophrenia and the Family*. New York: International Universities Press.

Link, N. F.; Scherer, S.; and Byrne, P. 1978. *Psychiatric News* 13(8):24.

Loewald, H. 1962. Internalization, separation, mourning, and the superego. *Psycho-analytic Quarterly* 31:483–504.

————. 1972. Freud's conception of the negative therapeutic reaction, with comments on instinct theory. *Journal of the American Psychoanalytic Association* 20(2):235–45.

London, N. 1978. Discussion of "transitional relatedness as a developmental line." Paper presented at the Spring meeting of the American Psychoanalytic Association, Atlanta, Georgia.

Lorenz, K. 1965. *Evolution and Modification of Behavior.* Chicago: University of Chicago Press.

MacLean, P. 1964. Man and his animal brains. *Modern Medicine* 32:95–106.

McDonald, M. 1970. Transitional tunes and musical development. *Psychoanalytic Study of the Child* 25:503–20.

Mahler, M.; Pine, F.; and Bergman, A. 1975. *The Psychological Birth of the Human Infant: Symbiosis and Individuation.* New York: Basic Books.

May, R. 1972. *Power and Innocence: A Search for the Sources of Violence.* New York: W. W. Norton & Co.

Modell, A. H. 1961. Denial and the sense of separateness. *Journal of the American Psychoanalytic Association* 9:533–47.

————. 1963. Primitive object relationships and the predisposition to schizophrenia. *International Journal of Psycho-Analysis* 44:282–92.

————. 1968. *Object Love and Reality: An Introduction to a Psychoanalytic Theory of Object Relations.* New York: International Universities Press.

————. 1970. The transitional object and the creative act. *Psychoanalytic Quarterly* 39:240–50.

Murphy, J. 1976. Psychiatric labeling in cross-cultural perspective. *Science* 191:1019–28.

Natterson, J. M. 1976. The self as a transitional object: its relationship to narcissism and homosexuality. *International Journal of Psychoanalysis and Psychotherapy* 5:131–44.

O'Neill, E. 1964. *The Plays of Eugene O'Neill.* New York: Random House.

Ornstein, P. 1975. On narcissism: beyond the introduction. In *Annual of Psychoanalysis,* vol. 2. New York: International Universities Press for the Chicago Institute for Psychoanalysis.

Pavenstedt, E., ed. 1967. *The Drifters.* Boston: Little, Brown & Co.

Piaget, J. 1932. *The Moral Judgment of the Child.* New York: Free Press, 1965.

————. and Inhelder, B. 1969. *The Psychology of the Child.* New York: Basic Books.

Plato. *Republic.* New York: Random House.

————. *Symposium*. In W. Kaufman, ed., *Philosophic Classics*. Englewood Cliffs, N.J.: Prentice-Hall, Inc., 1961.

Provence, S., and Ritvo, S. 1961. Effects of deprivation on institutionalized infants: disturbances in development of relationships to inanimate objects. *Psychoanalytic Study of the Child* 16:189–204.

————, and Lipton, R. C. 1962. *Infants in Institutions*. New York: International Universities Press.

Ritvo, S. 1971. Late adolescence: developmental and clinical considerations. *Psychoanalytic Study of the Child* 26:241–63.

Rizzuto, A. M. 1979. *The Birth of the Living God*. Chicago: University of Chicago Press.

Rolland, R. 1913. *Jean Christophe*. New York: Henry Holt & Co.

Rudhe,L., and Ekecrantz, L. 1974. Transitional phenomena: the typical phenomenon and its development. *Acta Psychiatrica Scandinavica* 50:381–400.

Russell, B. 1957. *Bertrand Russell: Why I am Not a Christian*. New York: Simon & Schuster.

Salzman, L. 1953. The psychology of religious and ideological conversion. *Psychiatry* 16:177–87.

Schafer, R. 1968. *Aspects of Internalization*. New York: International Universities Press.

————. 1976. *A New Language for Psychoanalysis*. New Haven, Conn.: Yale University Press.

Searles, H. F. 1976. Transitional phenomena and therapeutic symbiosis. *International Journal of Psychoanalysis and Psychotherapy* 5:145–204.

Shaw, G. B. 1947. *Back to Methuselah*. New York: Oxford University Press.

Solomon, J. C. 1962. The fixed idea as an internalized transitional object. *American Journal of Psychotherapy* 16:632–44.

Spitz, R. 1965. *The First Year of Life*. New York: International Universities Press.

Steinbeck, J. 1970. *East of Eden*. New York: Bantam Books.

Stevenson, O. 1954. The first treasured possession: a study of the part played by specially loved objects and toys in the lives of certain children. *Psychoanalytic study of the Child* 9:199–217.

Stoller, R. 1976. Sexual excitement. *Archives of General Psychiatry* 33:899–909.

Stone, L. 1967. The psychoanalytic situation and transference. *Journal of the American Psychoanalytic Association* 15:3–58.

Tolpin, M. 1971. On the beginnings of a cohesive self. *Psychoanalytic Study of the Child* 26:316–52.

Vaillant, G. E. 1971. Theoretical hierarchy of adaptive ego mechanisms. *Archives of General Psychiatry* 24:107–18.

Van Doren, M. 1975. *The Portable Emerson.* New York: Viking Press.

Volkan, V. 1972. The linking objects of pathological mourners. *Archives of General Psychiatry* 27:215–21.

Wagner, C. 1976. *Cosima Wagner's Diaries, 1869–1877.* New York: Harcourt Brace Jovanovich/Helen and Kurt Wolff Book.

Wagner, R. 1892–93. *Richard Wagner's Prose Works.* Vol. 2. New York: Broude Bros.

Winnicott, D. W. 1953. Transitional objects and transitional phenomena. *International Journal of Psycho-Analysis* 34:89–97.

———. 1965. *The Child, the Family and the Outside World.* Harmondsworth: Penguin Books.

———. 1971. Transitional objects and transitional phenomena. In *Playing and Reality.* New York: Basic Books, 1953.

———. 1977. *The Piggle.* New York: International Universities Press.

Wordsworth, W. Ode on intimations of immortality from recollections of early childhood. In *Wordsworth, Selected by Lawrence Durrell.* Baltimore: Penguin Books, 1973.

Index of Names and Titles

Index of Subjects